$\mathscr{F}$it for Excellence

Sheri Rose Shepherd

CREATION
HOUSE
Orlando, FL

FIT FOR EXCELLENCE by Sheri Rose Shepherd
Published by Creation House
Strang Communications Company
600 Rinehart Road
Lake Mary, Florida 32746
Web site: http://www.creationhouse.com

Unless otherwise noted, all Scripture quotations are from the New International Version of the Bible. Copyright © 1973, 1978, 1984, International Bible Society. Used by permission.

Scripture quotations marked KJV are from the King James Version of the Bible.

Scripture quotations marked NAS are from the New American Standard Bible. Copyright © 1960, 1962, 1963, 1968, 1971, 1972, 1973, 1975, 1977 by the Lockman Foundation. Used by permission.

Scripture quotations marked NLT are from the Holy Bible, New Living Translation. Copyright © 1996. Used by permission of Tyndale House Publishers, Inc., Wheaton, IL 60189. All rights reserved.

Scripture quotations marked NKJV are from the New King James Version of the Bible. Copyright © 1979, 1980, 1982 by Thomas Nelson, Inc., publishers. Used by permission.

Library of Congress Cataloging-in-Publication Data:
Shepherd, Sheri Rose, 1961–
    Fit for excellence / by Sheri Rose Shepherd.
        p. cm.
    Includes bibliographical references.
    ISBN: 0-88419-530-9 (pbk.)
    1. Weight loss—Religious aspects—Christianity. 2. Eating disorders—Religious aspects—Christianity. 3. Shepherd, Sheri Rose, 1961–
I. Title
RM222.2.S526 1998
248.8'6—dc21   98-4499
                                                                CIP

89012345 BBG 8765432
Printed in the United States of America

Excellent. A real blessing to me. Keep doing it and don't apologize for what you say. I have been in a rut with my weight, exercise, and diet. I am now motivated to resume with the idea I am fit for God.

—*Sharon R.*

Wonderful! Every female should listen to Sheri's testimony.

—*Debby C.*

Rich in the wisdom of the Word. Honest, straightforward presentation—a blessing!

—*Donna P.*

I have very much enjoyed Sheri Rose's ministry. Interesting, informative, encouraging, humorous, much needed.

—*Jacque D.*

Thank you for allowing God to use you to help us women understand the "TRUTH." How did we get so far from God's ways?

—*Cindy H.*

It was great! Straightforward, factual, needed to be said!

—*Renee B.*

I enjoyed your talk on nutrition. It's a message the church needs! I've been off sugar and white flour for four months now and feel great!

—*Michelle L.*

Wonderful! Food talk is especially helpful, new slant on reasons for healthy eating is refreshing to me.

—*Carolyn C.*

I learned a positive behavior for conquering everyday, persistent problems. It was not offensive to me. Thank you for sharing this valuable information.

—*Carol T.*

Acknowledgments

I'd like to thank those very special people who have made this ministry possible: Essentially Yours, Inc. (Brian, Barry, Geraldine, Jay, and Michel); Lana Krug; Duane and LeeAnn Rawlins; Phil Goodman; Layne Scharton; Joyce Wells; Tanna Behling; Susie Goodman; Paul Endrei; Carole Goodman; Larry Keefauver; Matt Jacobson; Dreamous Corporation (makers of Rejuvennis skin care); Christi O'Rourke; Randy Carlson; Todd Uddman; American Micro Products; Pierre Paroz; Hal and Susan Gooch; Jim and Tricia Richardson; Today's Family Life Communications; Parker and Cindy Grabill; the Shepherd family; Ken and Nancy Nair & Life Partners Christian Ministries; Brenda Ward; Tom Freiling and Creation House; Broadman & Holman; and Ingram Book Company.

To my Lord and Savior, Jesus Christ, who has given me the privilege of being a part of His work.

To my husband, Steve, for his sleepless nights co-writing this book with me and for standing beside me in some of my darkest hours.

To my little prince, Jacob. My most important ministry is you. I'm so blessed to have you as my son.

In Jeremiah 29:11, the Lord spoke this promise through Jeremiah to the Israelites just before He brought them out of captivity. "'For I know the plans I have for you,' declares the Lord, 'plans to prosper you and not to harm you, plans to give you hope and a future.'"

This book is to those who have lost hope, to those who are suffering as captives to a painful past, to the millions of women struggling with eating disorders or food addictions, to those who are too depressed and exhausted to enjoy life, and to those who are ready to live out God's call to excellence to finish this life strong . . . and win the crown of life.

—SHERI ROSE SHEPHERD
MRS. UNITED STATES, 1994

Contents

From the Heart

When this life is over, it won't matter what car we drove, what house we lived in, or how much money we made. The only thing that will matter is that we made a difference in somebody else's life.

I know from personal experience what it's like to grow up in what society refers to as a "dysfunctional home." (Today, there are so many dysfunctional families that much of the world has lost sight of what a healthy, functional family looks like.) My parents have been married and divorced three times each, and I've been a part of five blended families. My dad had an extremely violent temper, and my mom was paralyzed by emotional pain. Because they were always in one crisis situation after another, I never felt the freedom to go to my parents for comfort and direction. When I needed comfort, I found it in food. When I was in pain, I used drugs and alcohol to escape. By the time I was sixteen, I was addicted to both the food and the drugs. I had made so many poor choices, burned so many bridges, and nearly destroyed my mind and body. I believed I was destined for destruction. I wanted desperately to crawl out of this deep, dark hole of despair, but the harder I tried, the deeper I fell into depression.

At the lowest point in my life, my stepmom Susie challenged me with a painful question. She asked me how long I was going to use my past as an excuse for the poor choices I was making. She shocked me with the truth that I could do nothing to change my past, but I could choose to make the right choices to change my future.

That painful truth empowered me to change almost everything about myself. Believe it or not, in just one year, I lost all my weight, I stopped using drugs, I changed my friends, I changed my attitude, I improved my grades, I changed my clothes, my hair color, and while I was in a "change mode" I even changed my Jewish nose. (Daddy had a trade-out with a doctor!)

I went from a drug-using, overweight, insecure junior in high school to a powerful, popular senior who had boyfriends, a local beauty title, and a much better place in life. It looked like I had it all, and to the outside world I did. There was only one piece missing from what appeared to be the perfect puzzle: It didn't matter how much I projected a perfect life on the outside, because on the inside I continued to die a silent and secretive death that no one could see but me.

I followed my own personal success strategies, learned by carefully examining the latest research from all the top celebrities on television and in the magazines:

- Strategy #1: I had no basis for right and wrong . . . I just followed my feelings.
- Strategy #2: I bought things I didn't need to impress people I didn't really care about with money I didn't have.
- Strategy #3: I made excuses and blamed others because it was easier than accepting responsibility for my own actions.

- Strategy #4: I refused to forgive those who had hurt me, and I held on to bitterness and resentment.
- Strategy #5: My problems, my happiness, my success, and my entertainment consumed me.
- Strategy #6: I was anxious for everything and let all my requests be known to anyone who would listen.

My personal success strategies left me emotionally starving, lonely, and depressed because money, things, worldly success, and beauty could only hide my pain . . . they could not heal it!

Proverbs 14:12 says, "There is a way that seems right to a man, but in the end it leads to death." My life was a book with a sleek and colorful cover, but inside the pages were empty. Each chapter of what looked like my new life had the same title, "I'll Be Happy When . . . "

An English teacher of mine was so frustrated with me that she told me I would never amount to anything in life and that I was born to be a loser. I was certain my teacher was right until I discovered God's grammar lesson for broken lives like mine. God's grammar lesson teaches us not to put a period where He has a comma, because He has a plan for every life He creates.

By the time I reached age twenty-four, I did not know how to deal with my feelings. How could I possibly tell anyone that the young woman who seemed to have it all still cried herself to sleep every night, just like she did when she was a little girl. If I went to a doctor for my emotional pain, he would look at my blessed life and give me a drug for depression. I couldn't tell my parents because they were still dealing with their own problems, and I didn't want to tarnish their image of me. If I told my friends about my emotional pain, they would look at my successes and think that I was ungrateful. I certainly didn't want to pay some psychiatrist to pretend that he cared about me. So, I did what I had learned to do as a young girl; once again I ignored the warning signs. I covered them up by losing more weight, winning more pageants, making more money, setting more goals, and filling my schedule with excessive busyness so I wouldn't have time to feel any pain.

Then, at age twenty-four, I was again thrown back out on the road of reality. This time my emotional pain was so severe that every part of my body was hurting. I had panic attacks, crying spells, loss of memory, and chronic depression. The original pain from my childhood that had given me the power to change my life as a teenager no longer worked.

I had no more strength or desire to fill the empty pages of my life. I felt as if I were at the end of the story of my life. I could not decorate the pain I was feeling anymore. I thought out a way I could end my life quickly; I felt it would be better to die with the world thinking that I was successful than to disappoint them with the truth that I was a mess. The next week, I checked myself into a hotel room and decided that I would kill myself with sleeping pills. When I walked into the room, I threw myself on the floor and screamed at the top of my lungs, "God, do You exist? If You do, please show me!" As I lay there, face down on the floor, God revealed Himself to me through a vision of a long-forgotten friend named Allen, a drug dealer from my high school.

It was on a Friday in the field across from our school where Allen sold me drugs practically every day. On that cool California morning, Allen said he wouldn't be seeing me at any of the parties that weekend. He was going to some special weekend retreat with a friend. On Monday morning, I hurried to the field to buy my drugs before school, and there stood Allen. I remembered the look in his eyes, the smile on his face, the tenderness of his voice, and the wisdom of his words as he began to tell me about a loving God who had changed his life over the weekend. He said he no longer needed drugs to hide his pain because this God had healed him from the inside-out.

As I lay there on the floor, I started to wonder, *Could the same God change my life?* Then I remembered what Allen had told me. He said that God was the Author of my life and that He knew me better than I knew myself. Then he said, "Whenever you are ready to call on His name, He will be waiting. It doesn't matter where you've been, what you've done, or how you're feeling; He will accept you just as you are." It was hard for me to believe that all I had to do was call on the name of Jesus, and He would heal my hurts and give me a new life.

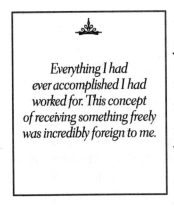

Everything I had ever accomplished I had worked for. This concept of receiving something freely was incredibly foreign to me.

Because of my Jewish up-bringing I was afraid to call on Jesus. So I called out to God and said, "God, if You exist and have a plan for my life, please reveal it to me." Then, after years of searching and trying everything else, this Jewish-American princess fell to her knees and called out on the name of Jesus . . . and found the peace and purpose for which she was so desperately looking.

"You will seek me and find me when you seek me with all your heart. I will be found by you," declares the LORD, "and will bring you back from captivity."
—JEREMIAH 29:13–14

He turned to me and heard my cry. He lifted me out of the pit of despair, out of the mud and the mire. He set my feet on solid ground.
—PSALM 40:1–2, NLT

I no longer search for a crown appointed by man. I have been given the greatest crown of all, the crown of life appointed by God. A crown that gives me something the world can never give—peace. My life makes sense. God now uses my pain for a purpose—to bless and encourage others. I have a renewed passion for people and a God-given power to live out my passions and let go of the pains from my past. My past no longer torments me. Instead, I have learned a valuable lesson about life. The truth is that life is hard . . . *but God is good.*

- He is strong in our weakness.
- He is comfort when we're in pain.
- He is love when we need acceptance.
- He is peace when we're haunted by fear.
- He is protection when we're in trouble.
- He heals our wounds when someone or something has hurt us.
- He is our joy when our hearts are grieved.
- He is our friend when we've been rejected.
- He is our power when we need a miracle.

His plan is the key to being set free from depression, food addictions, eating disorders, and emotional pain. He whom the Son has set free *is free indeed!*

1

The Crown

Since the beginning of time, men and women have searched for meaning and fulfillment in life. Eve must have thought she would find it in the wisdom from a pretty apple. Adam must have thought he would find it in pleasing pretty Eve. Just what is "it"? What is mankind searching for?

I have had the privilege of meeting people from all walks of life: people with fame and fortune; people who are lost and lonely; people who are intellectual, interesting, and intriguing; people who are powerful; and people who are beautiful. But no matter where I have walked in life, I have found a common goal existing in every heart—the search for fulfillment and peace of mind.

Where is a deep sense of satisfaction or rest for our anxious souls found? Is it in a pain-free world or the pursuit of pleasure? Or perhaps in a problem-free life or a perfect environment? How about the fleeting flame of passion or the tranquil bliss of solemn meditation? While all of these things may be wonderfully enticing, they can only give us external peace and temporary satisfaction. Because no matter what surrounds us, our souls long for *internal* peace . . . the peace that is only found in God.

> I am come that they might have life, and that they might have it more abundantly.
> —JOHN 10:10, KJV

An abundant life of peace and fulfillment *is* available. In fact, the reason Jesus made His humble entrance into humanity is to offer us abundance and eternity . . . the crown of life!

I have received "worldly" crowns, but to win each of them *I had to enter the race!* Unlike competitions in the world, when you enter the race for the crown of life, you've already won! The victory is already yours!

Can you imagine walking through life knowing that you've already won? Knowing that you are on the right path and that at the end of that path is a crown that already has your name on it? And even better, *you don't have to walk the path alone!* You can invite Jesus to walk with you. When the obstacles come, He'll be with you. When the storms hit, He'll protect you. And when you think you can't go on, He'll carry you. All you have to do is ask.

> Blessed is the man who perseveres under trial, because when he has stood the test, he will receive the crown of life that God has promised to those who love him.
> —JAMES 1:12

A SPIRIT-TO-SPIRIT RELATIONSHIP

God wants to have a Spirit-to-spirit relationship with you—not just an intellectual one—although many have settled for that. Many are "acquainted" with God by hearing others talk about Him or perhaps by occasionally reading the Bible. They simply don't understand that God wants to give them so much more.

In fact, some of the most brilliant men and women in all the world have missed out on discovering their human spirit and the opportunity to have Spirit-to-spirit relationships with the Creator of the universe! Even Nicodemus, one of the most intellectually gifted religious leaders of his day, could not grasp it. When Jesus told him he must be born again in order to enter the kingdom of God, Nicodemus shook his head in confusion—he was thinking and reasoning only in physical terms. Jesus responded by saying, "That which is born of the flesh is flesh; and that which is born of the Spirit is spirit" (John 3:6, KJV).

So what does this relationship with God look like?

If you and I wanted to know more about Tom Cruise, we could go to Beverly Hills and take a guided tour that stops in front of his house. We could even read about all the juicy details of his life in the magazines. But imagine if we were touring Tom's house and he actually opened the door and invited you in to visit with Nicole and the kids. That would be entirely different. You would be forming a relationship with the Cruise family. (Now, back to reality!) Have you ever toured the house of God? Probably. Ever read about Him? Heard those awesome Red Sea stories? Maybe. But do you understand that God Himself has invited you inside? That He loves you and wants to have a relationship with you?

God loves you and wants to live inside you and through you. When you open your spirit to Him, you'll discover that He longs to touch your every hurt, heal your deepest pain, revive your fainting heart, and soar with you over every mountain.

THE PATH

My dad had a satellite dish at his home in San Diego. It was ten feet across and could pick up every video broadcast known to man. Every May, he would call me on the phone just before I would sit down to watch the national telecast of the Miss USA Beauty Pageant. Without fail, he would predict which contestants would be selected for the top ten. Halfway through the telecast he would call me back and tell me that he had a "gut feeling" that Miss "So-and-So" was going to win. He drove me crazy, until I figured out that his satellite dish was picking up the video signals an hour before I was! (He was such a sneak!) Now, when I sit down to watch a nationally televised pageant, I know not to answer the phone!

Just like my dad's satellite receiver, we each have a satellite dish of sorts within us. God has wired us to be "tuned in" to basically two channels—the physical and the spiritual. The "physical channel" operates through our brain, and we respond mechanically or intellectually; the "spiritual channel" operates through our heart, and we respond emotionally. Unfortunately, it is more natural for us to respond to life by developing and nourishing only our mental and intellectual capabilities. So, likewise, it's natural to believe that our success in work, school, socially, and relationally depends entirely on our intellect, and when we can't make mental sense of it all, we grow frustrated, depressed, lonely, and unfulfilled.

We are made in the image of God, and our human spirit is designed to be a *reflection of God!* What an exciting thought! However, our minds don't *naturally* think about God or the things of the Spirit, so we end up being a rather "tainted" image. We just can't seem to help it! Like a moth is drawn to the flame, our thoughts naturally "tune in" to the physical or "sinful" nature and the desires of the flesh. To be truly fit for excellence, we cannot continue down that path.

We must take God's path, the Path of Excellence, and change our primary focus from the physical to the spiritual. If not, we experience two inevitable consequences.

1. *We miss out on a relationship with God and the power of being led by His Spirit* to do awesome things in this life that are pleasing to Him *and* fulfilling to us. Just as the branches of a vine will

dry up and wither if they are not connected to the vine, we too must remain in the vine if we are to grow and "bear fruit." (See John 15:5.) How sad it is to rely only on our own mental strength and wisdom and miss out on the spiritual wisdom of an infinite Creator!

2. *We miss out on eternity with Him.* Romans 8:6 says, "If your sinful nature controls your mind, there is death. But if the Holy Spirit controls your mind, there is life and peace" (NLT).

This book is about choosing God's path—the Path of Excellence—the path that leads to everlasting life!

Rest Stop

1. Are you walking on the Path of Excellence, or are you headed down your own path?

2

Observe the Warning Signs!

As you are trying to walk the Path of Excellence, have you ever been told you're too emotional? Or have you heard Christians say, "Emotions are ungodly; you need to ignore your feelings and live by faith"? Do you wonder why, then, did God give you emotions in the first place, if you are supposed to ignore them?

Perhaps you have asked yourself, "If God loves me, why am I feeling such pain?" Let me assure you that there is nothing wrong with your emotions. Emotions were designed by God for a reason. God does love you. He designed you to feel because you are created in His image—and the almighty God feels! Did you know there are more than two thousand instances in the Bible that refer to the emotions of God?

It seems obvious why a loving God would create positive emotions like joyfulness, peacefulness, excitement, and confidence, but why would unpleasant and negative emotions like loneliness, grief, rejection, despair, anger, and frustration be a part of His creative plan for us? Can we assume that they are just part of the curse of sin?

No. Because emotions, both positive and negative, were created by God to reveal the condition of the human spirit— a "warning sign" that something is wrong. Just as physical pain reveals that there is something wrong with our body, our emotions are a warning signal that something needs attention in our spirit. Ephesians 4:26 says, "Be angry, and do not sin" (NKJV). The sin isn't in feeling angry (or fearful or disgusted or anguished); the anger leads to sin when it isn't dealt with properly and reflects an ungodly behavior (an attitude or action).

If you've ever burned your hand on a stove, you probably didn't condemn your hand for feeling pain. "You stupid hand! It's just a red-hot stove! You shouldn't be hurting that bad!" The pain itself isn't the culprit. The pain is just the *evidence* of a damaging action. Would the pain be any less severe if you put your hand on the stove than it would be if someone else forced it there? Of course not. The effect is still the same. Whether you are the cause or not, you are still the victim! Likewise, the emotional pain we feel doesn't choose sides between right and wrong or good and bad. The cause of the emotion may or may not be sinful, but the effect is still the same—it hurts.

WARNING SIGNS

As you travel along the Path of Excellence, God has placed warning signs for you along the way. Watch carefully! They were lovingly placed there for a reason—and they may keep you from falling into one of life's big "ruts" on your journey.

Warning! Listen! Your spirit is speaking!

Women are notorious for beating themselves up with guilt for being "too emotional." We can't understand why we feel the way we do, we're told we shouldn't feel the way we do, and then we convince ourselves that the powerful emotions we're experiencing must stem from some flaw in our character! We then condemn ourselves like a poor hand burned by the red-hot stove. What a burden it is to carry that kind of guilt heaped unmercifully on top of our already heavy emotions. If you've been in bondage to this kind of guilt, you can take great comfort in this wonderful truth: It is impossible to be too emotional!

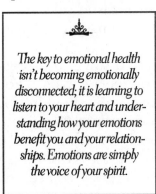

The key to emotional health isn't becoming emotionally disconnected; it is learning to listen to your heart and understanding how your emotions benefit you and your relationships. Emotions are simply the voice of your spirit.

Take a moment to reflect on a favorite movie. Many times we don't think about it, but the musical score plays a critical role; it adds life, dimension, and vibrant color to each scene. Sometimes its foreboding, ominous theme warns of looming danger. In the next scene it might enhance the beauty of a romantic embrace or reflect the sorrow of love swept away in death. To hit the mute button during a heart-pounding, climactic finish would be a crime!

•••••••••••••••••••••••••••••

Rest Stop

1. Do you feel guilty for revealing your emotional pain to others? How about to God?

2. Consider a conflict in your life. In what ways were your emotions involved? How did you deal with them?

Warning! You may be experiencing emotional pain!

Whether you realize it or not, you may be in emotional

pain. Not sure? Do you recognize any of these symptoms?

- Do you live in your past and worry about your future?
- Are you depressed and feeling empty inside?
- Do you feel defeated because of a poor self-image?
- Are you in bondage to other people's opinions of you?
- Do you take everyone's stress personally or fall apart when someone looks at you the wrong way?
- Do you keep yourself excessively busy to the point that your life feels out of control?
- Do you have compulsive behavior patterns?
- Do you feel guilty for saying *no,* even if you've done it for the right reasons?
- Are you paralyzed by fear?
- Do you have a short fuse? How do you react to disappointment?
- Do you have a history of destructive relationships?
- Are you an approval addict?

....
Rest Stop

1. Is there someone or something who has hurt you deeply? What emotions can you identify that have resulted from that hurt? Pray that God will help you identify them.

2. Do you recognize any of the above symptoms of emotional pain? If so, which ones? How do they affect you?

Warning! Heed the six "Don'ts"!

If you are suffering from emotional pain, pay attention to the six "Don'ts" of emotional fitness:

- *Don't ignore it!* Ignoring the warning signs will not make them go away any more than ignoring a gas tank that says "empty" will allow the car to continue to run.
- *Don't excuse it!* Many of us make excuses for our emotional pain rather than looking at the problem that's causing it.
- *Don't decorate it!* Many times we decorate our pain with pretty houses, pretty clothes, and prestigious positions.
- *Don't cover it up!* Many of us cover up with accomplishments and excessive busyness.
- *Don't pretend it's not there!* Many of us have no idea why we're feeling pain because we pretend that everything is okay.
- *Don't postpone dealing with it!* Don't postpone dealing with your warning signs, or they will deal with you.

Rest Stop

1. Which one of the six "Don'ts" best demonstrates the way you handle emotional pain in your life?

2. Are you currently handling any emotional pain in that way today?

3. Could God be speaking to you through your emotions? In what way?

Warning! Denial ahead!

If you don't deal with your emotional pain, it will deal with you, your loved ones, and your life. Pretending it doesn't exist won't help you get emotionally fit. I pretended that my pain didn't exist for so long that I earned my doctorate degree in denial.

When a warning light comes on in a car, putting a piece of black tape over the warning light won't fix the car. When a car is broken, it needs to be taken to a mechanic, one who knows how the car works and understands how to fix it. Some people drive through life ignoring all the warning lights until one day they find themselves broken down in a ditch somewhere. Don't wait—fix it now!

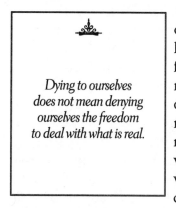

Dying to ourselves does not mean denying ourselves the freedom to deal with what is real.

I didn't deal with my pain. I covered up my warning signs. My life did break down, and I was forced to face my feelings the night I almost lost my life to a drug overdose. The emotional roller coaster I lived on warned me of danger, but I didn't know what to do or where to turn. It wasn't long before I derailed and crashed. Suddenly, I was thrown onto a road of reality. I had to face the fact that I was a drug-addicted, D-student, self-destructive teenager going no-where in life. I had to "get real" with who I was and who I was becoming. A few years later, I did finally get real with God.

If we deny or stuff these emotions, we will never be emotionally fit. Some of us think that being spiritual requires denying how we really feel.

If we are not honest about our emotions, covering up the warning signals of our spirit, we will slowly die inwardly. God is a God of truth—and only the truth can set you free. I'm not saying that you should tell the whole world all your problems, but I am saying to tell them to God, the mighty Counselor.

If you are having trouble identifying what you are really feeling and why it's affecting you, pray and ask God to show you the hidden hurts that need to be healed. Come out of the shadows into His glorious light and be set free to fly!

> Then you will know the truth, and the truth will set you free.
>
> —JOHN 8:32

Do you ever tell Him about your anger, bitterness, jealousy, resentment, or hatred? Sounds ungodly, doesn't it? Have you ever thought to yourself: *I shouldn't be feeling this way? Why can't I be joyful about this?*

It's time to get real with God. Voice to God your bitterness, your jealousy, your envy, your hatred, and your resentment. Many times we tell everybody but God how we feel. Sometimes when we try to handle our pain by ourselves, we are playing our own God. He loves us no matter what emotions we are dealing with.

Sounds ungodly, doesn't it? But it's not. He sees behind the curtain that covers your heart. Don't give a false performance for God. Invite Him into the dark room where you hide your pain. He promises to be your strength when you're too weak. He will be a light in your darkness. Don't hide the emotions in your heart—they're the voice of your spirit. Confess them to God, and ask Him to give you His strength to walk in the Spirit and not in the flesh.

The Scripture doesn't say, "Be anxious for everything and let all your requests be known by anyone who will listen." It says, "Be anxious for nothing, but in everything by prayer and supplication, with thanksgiving, let your requests be made known to God" (Phil. 4:6, NKJV).

In the fifth chapter of the Gospel of Mark, there's an example of a woman who knew exactly to whom to turn in time of trouble. This example of physical suffering and the steps that brought her healing apply to the emotional pain you may be experiencing today.

1. *She knew she needed healing.*

The bleeding this poor woman experienced could not be hidden. For twelve years she was ceremonially unclean, and every thing and every one she touched each day was made unclean. She was way past the stage of "this suffering I feel is no big deal." She had obviously confessed her need and reached a point of desperation. If you're going to move out of denial and get real with God, face your need head-on and move beyond *suppression* to *confession.*

2. *She tried everything else.*

The Bible says that not only was this woman victimized by this ailment for twelve years, but she literally spent all that she had on professional remedies—only to discover that she was getting worse! Do you need to acknowledge that your own efforts and worldly treatments are just not going to be strong enough to heal you? Perhaps you haven't exhausted all of your human effort. This poor woman had to wait twelve years before she had the chance of a lifetime for healing. It took her twelve years to "take hold" of Jesus. How long will it take you?

3. *She didn't care what people thought.*

When you want to get healed badly enough, you'll "fight the crowds" to pursue it. If, for example, you had a physical ailment like severe chest pains, you would tell someone right away, wouldn't you? Of course you would. But most people, even in churches, are too embarrassed or ashamed to seek help for emotional suffering. In the Gospel of Mark, the suffering woman wasn't just in physical pain. She must have felt deep emotional pain as well. Because she was "unclean" according to the Law, she was literally a social outcast from her friends and family and from worshiping in the temple. The pain her spirit felt from rejection must have been unbearable. Yet, do you think any embarrassment or pride or condemnation from others was going to keep her away from her Healer? The crowd was pressing in around Jesus from all sides. There was a frenzied stampede of Jesus fans. But one frail, wounded lady let nothing stop her. What is keeping you from your Healer today?

4. *She discovered acceptance and understanding of her frailty and experienced the power of Jesus.*

"If I could just touch the hem of His garment, I would be healed." What faith she had! She had no more money. She had no more friends. She had no more strength. She had no more answers. She had no more self-confidence. But with faith . . . she had no more obstacles!

Jesus knows and understands your pain, and He accepts you in your frail condition. When your little bit of faith lays hold of the power of Jesus, He is able to grant you peace and freedom—and, in His time, healing.

·······················
Rest Stop

1. Can you recognize whether you have denied or hidden your feelings? Why?

2. Write out your hurts and the emotions you've felt in a prayer to God.

3. Try to discover what He wants you to learn in each hurt.

Warning! Storms ahead!

Maybe God has been trying to get your attention. He's speaking to your spirit. He's designed your emotions to serve as warning signs beckoning you to higher ground. "Don't Go There! Turn Back."

I'm learning that not every storm that comes my way is God's plan. Maybe you're in a painful storm right now, and God is beside you, guiding you through. Or, maybe He has posted warning signs in your path: "Danger! Bridge Out! Do Not Cross When Flooded!" Storms will come, not to teach us to run, but to help us take root more firmly.

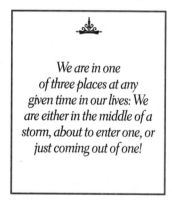

We are in one of three places at any given time in our lives: We are either in the middle of a storm, about to enter one, or just coming out of one!

My friend Tracy found herself in this predicament. Before her wedding, sitting in her bridal gown in a quiet corner of an unfamiliar church, she pleaded with God to show her if she was doing the right thing marrying this man. His controlling spirit and abusive behavior left her feeling worthless and rejected. Yet, she lacked the courage to escape.

In her book, *The Courage to Say No More,* Tracy recalled that God had indeed answered her prayers. Countless times God had warned her that this was a storm she did not have to go through. Although she didn't understand at the time, her intense emotional pain had been screaming incessantly from within her for months, "This is not right! Turn back!"

In that quiet corner of the church, she wiped her tears, stuffed her feelings, and responded to the voice within her, "I don't." At the altar two hours later, she stood in the presence of five hundred witnesses and a drunken groom and said, "I do." When it comes to storms, each of us needs to be aware of the forecast.

Don't be discouraged. God wants to help you by either steering you clear from struggles ahead or by holding you tightly to Himself and taking you through them. In either case, when God is doing the steering, it will always be for your good if you love Him and are called according to His purpose. Mistakes are the tutors that make us wiser.

I no longer look to man to find the perfect life; rather I look to God to find perfect peace. I am no longer afraid to go through the storms of life because I know God can calm any storm. I also know that sometimes it's better for our emotional health for Him to calm His child in the midst of a storm so we can learn to rest in Him when the storms of life hit hard.

James 1:2–3 says, "Whenever trouble comes your way, let it be an opportunity for joy. For when your faith is tested, your endurance has a chance to grow" (NLT).

....
Rest Stop

1. Looking back on your life, what storms has God brought you through? What have you learned from them?

2. What storms are in your life right now that you need to give to God? Write a prayer, giving them to God.

3. What storms can you see ahead that God wants to steer you clear of?

4. Can you identify any coming storms that you are sensing God would like to bring you through?

5. Keeping in mind God's plan to strengthen you and help you grow, can you identify how these "troubles" accomplish that in your life?

3

Don't Get Stuck in an Emotional Rut

All my life my dad has told me how much he loved me. I knew in my heart that he did. Probably more than anything else in his life. However, he had a horrible temper, and when it exploded, he would verbally abuse me with words that would crush my spirit. When he was done with his temper tantrum, he would remind me how much he loved me. This made me very confused about what love was supposed to look or feel like. Now that I'm an adult, I realize that he loved me to the best of his ability, but it was a toxic love; it made my heart sick with emotional pain.

THE RUT OF EMOTIONAL PAIN

Emotional pain is a great big lonely rut on life's path! But if you want to continue your journey on the Path of Excellence, you must get out! After all, just how rewarding can life be when the rut you are in is so deep that you can't even enjoy the scenery along the way?

Climbing out of a rut hurts. But just as getting real with

17

God and telling Him your hidden hurts brings healing, *so does getting out of the ruts of emotional pain that are destroying your health.*

While you are climbing out of the ruts and starting on a new path, don't get discouraged if at the beginning you feel like your pain is getting worse. When you stop putting junk food into your physical body, the body has to get rid of the toxins in order to build healthy cells. While the body is detoxing, it will feel sicker at first.

The same is true with your emotions. When you're letting go of the emotional "junk" in your life, you may experience more pain in the beginning. You've denied and hidden your pain for so long that when you start on a healthier path, it feels foreign.

Be encouraged; this pain is only temporary when you take the necessary steps to get rid of those toxins. But understand, it's not always easy. As you go through these steps you will have to fight your flesh to do what's right! Scripture tells us that our flesh wages a battle against the spirit. (See Romans 7.) But take heart—the greater your battle, the greater your victory will be!

When Jesus was in the Garden of Gethsemane, about to go to the cross to be crucified, He was in such emotional pain that He was greatly troubled, even grieved to the point of death. His sweat fell like drops of blood. (See Luke 22:44.) In pure agony, He asked His Father in heaven, "Is there any way this cup can be passed from Me?" In other words, He was asking God, "Is there another way . . . an easier way?"

As we know, there was not an easier way. He had to experience the loneliness . . . the rejection . . . the suffering. The emotional and physical pain were part of the burden He willingly bore when He took our place and paid the penalty for our sins.

The victory He won came at an incredible price. His agonizing death finally completed what God had been trying to do since the Garden of Eden: His pain, His death, restored the broken relationship between a loving and holy God and His rebellious children—not for a moment, or for a day, but for eternity!

Have you ever felt as if your rut of emotional pain were so great that you grieved to the point of death? Or cried for a way out? Do you hide it from God? Don't . . . because Jesus didn't. Crying out to God with a broken heart guarantees His presence in your pain. He lives with those who have a broken and lowly spirit. (See Isaiah 57:15.)

Perhaps one of the hardest things for you to do is to admit that you're in emotional pain. You may deny it, despise it, and decorate it, but rarely take the time to understand it as the voice of your human spirit.

THE RUT OF SHAME

When Adam ate the fruit of the tree, his sin left him with an emotional burden called *shame*. What did he do when the voice of his spirit cried out from this strange new emotional pain? He ran and hid himself from God, then he defended himself by blaming Eve.

When Jesus, the second Adam, hung crucified on the tree, our sin left Him with an emotional burden called *shame*. What did Jesus do when His spirit cried out from this undeserved emotional pain? He willingly bore the pain of our sorrow, our grief, our shame, and our sin . . . yet He opened not His mouth in defense.

If you feel lonely and rejected, or fearful and ashamed, what do you do with your emotional pain? You may have been afflicted by the unloving blows of another person or maybe by your own disobedience.

Whatever the cause, you don't have to feel guilty for crying out to God. When you do cry out, you are identifying with Jesus. You are learning to know Him and the fellowship of His suffering. When you hide out, you are identifying with Adam and separating yourself from the sweet fellowship of God.

The pain Jesus felt brought us eternal healing and restoration. His suffering brought us into fellowship. God wants us to experience that fellowship by sharing our pain with Him and with other believers. The result is unity, restoration, strength, and yes, healing.

Just remember: The same resurrection power that raised Jesus from the dead will give you the power to deal with your pain and lead you to a more intimate relationship with Him! You'll be able to experience excellence in your life in a way you could never have dreamed possible.

There is no easy way to deal with emotional pain, but God promises that those who sow with tears will reap with joy. The same is true for you.

The Rut of Toxic Love

Do you have a spouse, a friend, or a parent who says he loves you . . . but you don't understand why this love hurts so badly? If so, you may be experiencing toxic love.

Have you ever taken a big bite out of a plum you thought was ripe and winced at the sour taste? Every cell in your mouth screamed out in defense, "Spit it out before you get sick!"

Our bodies were designed to warn us of potentially harmful things, like unripe fruit, in order to keep us from getting sick. In the same way, we recognize whether someone is led by the Spirit by how healthy the "fruit" is in his or her life. Healthy love is a natural product—or fruit—of the Spirit living inside us. "But the fruit of the Spirit is love . . . " (Gal. 5:22).

It may be difficult for you to understand the difference between healthy love and toxic love. After all, if you have only experienced toxic love, how can you even know what healthy love "looks" like? You must learn to recognize the warning signals of a love that is "not ripe" or toxic. This is one rut that can make your heart sick and lead to unhealthy, ungodly relationships.

Warning Signals of Toxic Love

Verbally assaulting	Codependent
No respect	Selfish
Takes advantage	Holds grudges
Controlling	Cruel
Jealous	Revengeful
Discouraging	Demanding
Guilt manipulative	Abusive
Dishonest	

RESPONDING TO TOXIC LOVE RELATIONSHIPS

One of the best examples in the Bible of how we should respond to toxic love is found in the life of Joseph. Joseph went through amazing trials in his life, and they all stemmed from his brothers' jealousy of him. First, they threw him in a pit with plans to kill him. They then sold him into slavery and told their dad that his favorite son was killed by a wild animal. Joseph then wound up in prison after being framed by his boss's wife. He finally got out of prison after two years because he interpreted the Pharaoh's dreams; he eventually rose to power in Egypt as Pharaoh's right-hand man. He even became a huge hero in the land by rescuing millions from a seven-year famine. The story really gets interesting, however, when we see how Joseph responds to his brothers when they come to Egypt for food. Read the story of Joseph in chapters 37–47 of Genesis. Here are some key steps I found from Joseph's response to his brothers' toxic love:

1. *He didn't deny the problem.*

Joseph knew his brothers had rejected him and had nothing but hateful, evil intentions for him. He didn't deny that they hurt him deeply. When he saw them years later, he didn't throw open his arms and accept them as if nothing had ever happened. You may be a victim of rejection or

21

abuse. Don't deny the problem! Don't deny the hurt!

If someone punches you in the eye and then later pleads for forgiveness with a sorrowful confession and heartfelt repentance, what do you think that's going to do for your eye? Suppose you show up at church two weeks later and a friend notices that you still have a black eye. "Didn't you forgive him?" your friend might say. "If you would forgive, your hurt would be gone! You know what they say, 'Forgive and forget!'" Pretty silly, wouldn't you say? It's the same with our emotions. Whether repentance and forgiveness are applied to the wound or not, *healing still takes time!*

2. *He kept God's agenda.*

Joseph knew that God had a plan for him, and he wasn't about to let anything destroy it, including his brothers. He knew his brothers' deceitful hearts, so he kept a cautious distance and tested their motives and the truth of their words. (See Genesis 42.) Just as God was with Joseph through his abuse and imprisonment, He will be with you and will turn what was intended for evil into good. However, *this does not mean you should abandon caution and open the door for more abuse!*

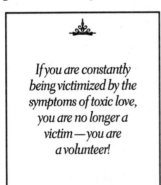

If you are constantly being victimized by the symptoms of toxic love, you are no longer a victim—you are a volunteer!

You cannot expect anyone else to value you if you don't value yourself! God values you so much that He sent His Son to die for you! You are valuable! But God doesn't want you to let someone else destroy your body (His temple) with emotional or physical abuse. Don't let them.

3. *He ministered reconciliation.*

Reconciliation means "to make things right or to restore a relationship." After protecting himself and God's purpose in his life from any additional harm, Joseph's final step was to minister reconciliation. He reached out with a pure heart of forgiveness because he saw that God's love and His purposes were bigger than his pain. The good news of God's love for us illustrates this principle through Jesus:

> Therefore if anyone is in Christ, he is a new creation; the old has gone, the new has come! All this is from God, who reconciled us to himself through Christ and gave us the ministry of reconciliation.
>
> —2 CORINTHIANS 5:17–18

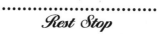

Rest Stop

1. List some unhealthy relationships in your life. What makes them unhealthy?

2. Can you recognize any of your emotional responses in these relationships? List them.

THE RUT OF UNFORGIVENESS

I'll never forget the pain I felt when I was pregnant with my son, Jacob. I really wanted my mother in my life. I hadn't seen her since my wedding, so I wrote a letter to her about my pregnancy. Not long after, on one hot summer day, I received a box in the mail from my mom. I was anxious to see what was inside and tore it open as quickly as I could. *Great!* I thought. *My mom sent a gift for the baby!* When I opened it, I was surprised to find my baby shoes, my old baby photos, and my birth certificate enclosed with an accompanying letter, which read, " . . . I wish you had never been born; you were one of the biggest mistakes I've ever made." That day I experienced a pain I could not escape. If

I did not deal with it, it would have affected my marriage and my motherhood. Through a bucket of tears, I sat down and wrote her a real letter—a letter that cut through the bitterness and loneliness that I know we had both felt for years. It was a letter asking forgiveness, and it paved the long road to healing.

It's worth losing the battle to win the war. Don't get in the rut of who's wrong and who's right. Do what you can do to make it right, than watch the healing begin in your heart.

GOD'S FORGIVENESS

Before we can even address the issue of unforgiveness, we must ask ourselves if we have understood and received God's forgiveness. Hebrews 10:10 says, "We have been made holy through the sacrifice of the body of Jesus Christ once for all." This means that God has assured us of absolute forgiveness for our sins so that the first step toward a whole relationship with God is done!

> For he has rescued us from the dominion of darkness
> and brought us into the kingdom of the Son he loves,
> in whom we have redemption, the forgiveness of sins.
> —COLOSSIANS 1:13

Is there a rut of unforgiveness in the path on which you are traveling? If so, it's time for you to get out . . . but how?

Step 1: Receive God's forgiveness.

Begin by receiving God's forgiveness for your sins. Ask Him to show you those people who have suffered as a result of your emotional damage. If you've spent years denying your emotional hurts, it has not only affected you; it has surely hurt those around you and built walls of separation. Has that separation led to bitterness, resentment, or anger?

Step 2: Go to the people you've hurt and ask them to forgive you.

Write, call, or do it in person. Don't postpone it. You cannot move to the next step of emotional healing until you do. Perhaps, like the prodigal son, you need to return home and ask forgiveness. Remember—if you refuse to make things right with those you have hurt, then how can you stand before God who has forgiven you? If those you have hurt refuse to forgive you, don't force them. Remember, pain takes time to heal. The best thing you can do is pray.

Step 3: Forgive those who have caused you pain.

If you think about God's incredible forgiveness, is it any wonder that He expects you to forgive others as well? Jesus shares this principle in a parable about a servant who begged forgiveness from his master because he could not repay a huge debt—millions of dollars in today's money. (See Matthew 18:23–25.) The master felt compassion for the servant and, believe it or not, forgave the entire debt! The servant then headed for home, still basking in gratefulness, when he came across a fellow servant who owed him some lunch money. Did he share with his friend the great news of his master's forgiveness? No way! He strangled him and insisted that he cough up the money immediately! He even threw him in jail until he could repay! Shouldn't he have shown mercy to his fellow servant? Jesus says *yes;* He even says that if we don't, our act of unforgiveness will actually stop the flow of God's forgiveness to us. If we really want to be healed, we must forgive.

I know how hard this can be from personal experience. I've had many people in my life hurt me, including my parents. When I was a little girl, I was starved for my mother's approval, but she refused to give it to me. She would always tell me how much better everyone else was than me, and because of this I thought for sure she didn't love me. My mother was a very unhappy person because she held on to bitterness and resentment toward her mother all her life. Because my mother did not deal with the unforgiveness in her life, that pain was passed on to me. I realized that I had a difficult time enjoying healthy relationships with women because I had unresolved, hidden hurts in my own heart. Out of self-protection, I found myself keeping a distance from my mother; pretty soon, she no longer wanted to have anything to do with me.

Forgiving someone doesn't mean that the pain automatically goes away. But it does uproot the bitterness and resentment in your heart that is preventing your healing.

Time does heal your broken heart—when you do things God's way.

It took seven more years after I wrote that letter to my mom for the pain to go away. Today, my mother and I have a loving, healthy relationship.

But what if someone's action toward you is also a sin against God? Again, Jesus said to forgive. However, this does not mean that you should make the mistake of carrying the heavy burden of making that person right with God. It is *their* responsibility to repent of their sinfulness to God. Lay that burden down before Him.

Step 4: Forgive yourself.

This step is usually the hardest. For some reason, we feel responsible or obligated to stay in this rut. But without forgiving yourself you can't become emotionally free, and you will remain frozen by your failures. *You can never change anything you have said or done in your past, but you can learn from it and let it go!*

Who could have a better reason for not forgiving himself than the apostle Peter? He had walked with Jesus, and his life had been changed forever by this friend. Yet when tough times hit, he denied that he had ever even known his friend—not once, but three times! Imagine if Peter had never forgiven himself for denying Jesus. If he had allowed his failures to paralyze him, he would never have finished God's call on his life . . . the call to be the "rock" upon which Christ would later build His church! (See Matthew 16:18.)

Forgive yourself today. Don't allow the enemy of your emotions to remind you of your sin. God has taken the load of sin and guilt off your back and has thrown it into the "sea of forgetfulness." You have no business hanging around the seashore with a fishing pole and a net trying to retrieve it. Leave it there and move on with God!

God tells us that He will forgive wickedness and will remember our sins no more (Isa. 43:25).

••••••••••••••••••••••••••••
Rest Stop

1. Write some examples of how the rut of unforgiveness has disrupted your life and your relationships.

2. Write out a prayer of confession to God, asking His help in this area.

THE RUT OF UNRIGHTEOUS ANGER

Have you ever been so angry that your face got red hot? That's exactly what the Hebrew word for *anger* means. The Bible is full of examples of this kind of burning anger. Have you ever been told you shouldn't feel angry? Is it ungodly? Did you know there are benefits to anger?

Anger is an emotion—designed by God—to reveal that your spirit has been attacked, provoked, or wounded. Our flesh (our ego—the selfish, sinful part of us) can also be provoked or exposed if it has not been put to death. (See Galatians 5:24.)

What we do with anger depends on whether we are being led by God's Spirit or by our flesh. If we are controlled by our flesh—our sinful nature—anger will trigger a sinful attitude or action. If we respond this way, we will fall into a dangerous rut that may cause extreme damage to ourselves and others physically, emotionally, and spiritually.

If, on the other hand, our spirit is led by God's Spirit, anger will still trigger a response, but this time God will be honored. Ephesians 4:26 says, "Be angry, yet do not sin; do not let the sun go down on your anger." Anger is not a sin, but we must do something with it before the sun goes down.

A prominent Christian leader told of a conference where he was speaking. In the front row of every session he taught, there sat a woman and her husband. The man struggled to stay awake during the conference, but by the middle of the day he was sleeping soundly—even snoring.

Needless to say, the Christian speaker was perturbed by this rude behavior, and he struggled with anger throughout the conference.

Immediately after the last session, Rip Van Winkle and his wife hastily approached the speaker

"Oh, we are so thrilled to finally meet you!" the wife gushed. "We enjoyed your speaking so much! We can't believe how blessed we are to be here! You see, my husband has a rare medical disorder, and his doctors have only given him a few more weeks to live. His last request was to fly wherever you are just to hear you speak!"

The well-known Christian leader was humbled and embarrassed by his attitude. His anger had revealed a lack of understanding.

> He who is slow to anger has great understanding, but
> he who is quick-tempered exalts folly.
> —PROVERBS 14:29, NAS

WHAT DO YOU DO WITH YOUR ANGER?

1. *Stop! Wait!* Make a conscious effort to acknowledge who's in control—your flesh or God's Spirit.
2. *Think the situation through.* To what are you reacting? Is your spirit being attacked or provoked? Or, is your flesh being exposed? Remember, our flesh refuses to die willingly. It will jump to defend itself at every opportunity.
3. *Look at the offender's heart.* Is there something you don't fully understand about this situation? Look at your own heart to make sure you are being controlled by God's Spirit.
4. *Admit your feelings to God.* Don't repress your anger. Ask God to give you understanding. Look for what God is trying to reveal about your own Spirit—or your flesh.
5. *Decide on the most appropriate action.* Jesus had complete understanding and acted righteously when His anger triggered an aggressive response causing Him to clear the money-changers and wicked merchants out of the Temple court. Perhaps you have lost a child in a drunk-driving accident; as a result, your anger may have motivated you to gain understanding and to get involved with Mothers Against Drunk Drivers.

Remember, it is okay to feel angry. Whether that anger triggers a sinful attitude or action is up to us.

Rest Stop

1. Do you remember the last time that you were really angry? What did you do with that anger?

29

2. List three situations that cause recurring anger in your life. Can you identify the role a lack of understanding plays in your anger?

3. What positive steps can you take now to solve them? Ask God to give you understanding.

THE RUT OF TOXIC GUILT

Contrary to pop psychology, guilt is not always bad. Guilt is an emotion that warns us when something about our thoughts or actions is "not quite right." But as with many emotions, guilt has become twisted. Many of us spend precious emotional energy dealing with toxic guilt.

Toxic guilt is the product of our accepting the responsibility for another's sinfulness as they shift the blame for their actions on us. Some of us take the responsibility for everything that goes wrong around us. Then, on top of that, we allow the devil or others to manipulate us to feel shame. We know that it feels bad inside, but what we don't recognize is that it feels that way because we are carrying a burden of blame *that's not ours to carry!*

The next time you're on the receiving end of a barrage of blame from someone, take a look at the one pulling the trigger. If the blame fired at you is through another person's hostile defensiveness, you may be a potential victim of toxic guilt. Watch out! Don't use this guilt on others, and don't receive it. It will steal your peace of mind and separate you from God. Don't pick up burdens that you're not called to carry!

CONVICTION

There is a guilt that is designed to help you along on your

path. It's the guilt you feel when you have done something wrong. It's conviction. It's a signal that warns you when you're falling off the path or have taken a wrong turn. This guilt is given to you by God's Spirit, and He will not remove it until you repent.

Repentance is not "simply saying you're sorry." It is actually turning away from whatever is causing you to sin. You can, however, ignore this guilt if you work at it hard enough. You can cover it up, you can justify it, or you can look the other way. Yet, you will *never experience emotional health until you learn to listen and respond to God's guilt with repentance.*

....
Rest Stop

1. Do you feel "God's guilt" in your life?

2. What do you need to repent from? Make it right today.

3. Ask God to reveal to you any toxic guilt that you are giving or receiving.

4. List any guilt issues.

5. What can you do to deal with these issues?

THE RUTS OF FEAR AND WORRY

As I reflect on my life, I'm amazed at how many things I worried about for no good reason. I've suffered many catastrophes in my life . . . most of which never happened! Jesus asked, "Can all your worries add a single moment to your life? . . . Your heavenly Father already knows all your needs, and he will give you all you need from day to day if you live for him and make the Kingdom of God your primary concern. So don't worry about tomorrow, for tomorrow will bring its own worries. Today's trouble is enough for today" (Matt. 6:27–34, NLT).

I used to have an incredible fear of flying . . . well, actually it was a fear of crashing! One day I was telling a godly man how much I feared flying. He asked me a very challenging question. He wanted to know if I believed that God was sovereign (ultimately in charge). It was at that moment I realized that if I believed that God was sovereign and if I believed that God loved me, I had nothing to fear.

Did you know that obsessive fears and worrying can be a way of avoiding unresolved issues and pain from deep inside? After all, if you spend all of your time obsessing about what may or may not happen, then you don't have any energy left to deal with what's *really* bothering you down deep. Obsessing can be easier than trusting, but obsessing keeps you apart from God.

Fear and worry are actually rooted in unbelief and are the antitheses of trust. Unfortunately, you may have never learned to trust. Perhaps you grew up with too few people in your life that you could depend on and believe. If so, trusting God is difficult for you. But without letting go and believing He can and will take care of you, you will be trapped in the rut of fear and worry forever. Ask yourself two questions:

1. *Do I believe You, God?* "Do not fear, for I am with you" (Isa. 41:10).

2. *Have I sought You?* "I sought the LORD and he answered me; he delivered me from all my fears" (Ps. 34:4).

Now, when I am in fear, I remember God's words of comfort, "If I am with you, who can be against you?" I reflect on Matthew 28:20 where Jesus says, "Be sure of this: I am with you always, even to the end of the age" (NLT).

The more I focus on the things of God, the less I fear the things of man. I find great strength in knowing that His perfect love casts out all fear.

When fear and worry start to paralyze me, I remember that God is the God of peace. We cannot know what is going to happen in life, but we can know Him. When we keep our eyes fixed on Him, we will find ourselves standing on a solid rock.

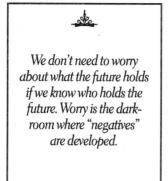

We don't need to worry about what the future holds if we know who holds the future. Worry is the darkroom where "negatives" are developed.

Don't worry about anything; instead, pray about everything. Tell God what you need and thank Him for all He has done. If you do this, you will experience God's peace, which is far more wonderful than the human mind can understand. His peace will guard your hearts and minds as you live in Christ Jesus. (See Philippians 4:6–7.)

- Worry steals your joy.
- Worry steals your today.
- Worry makes you mean . . . just ask your kids!

······························
Rest Stop

1. Make a list of everything you worry about.

2. Write your worries down in a prayer to God, and then leave them in His hands.

3. Make a list of some of your worst fears. Next to each fear, write down where this fear came from. Do you recognize any unbelief that may have caused it?

4. When David was running for his life out of fear, he finally "sought the Lord" and then experienced deliverance from his fear. Write a prayer of seeking, and then surrender your fears to God.

THE "PEOPLE-PLEASING" RUT

Do you constantly worry about what other people think? I used to be consumed about what others thought about me—almost every decision I made was based on what others might think! I finally realized that I could worry much less about what others think about me . . . if I just realized how seldom others actually think about me!

In an imperfect world, you cannot have and *do not need* every person's approval! If you calculate what you do and say because it will make you more popular with people, then you will be rendered ineffective to God. Paul asked, "Am I now trying to win the approval of men, or of God? Or am I trying to please men? If I were still trying to please men, I would not be a servant of Christ" (Gal. 1:10).

The only way to break this addiction is to look to God for your approval, not to others. You can either be a God-pleaser or a people-pleaser.

There is no peace riding the fence. (You'll get splinters in your tush!)

....
Rest Stop

1. Write some examples of how "people-pleasing" has disrupted your life and your relationships.

2. Write out a prayer to God of confession, asking for help in this area.

THE FINANCIAL RUT

Years ago, because of circumstances beyond our control, our production company was unable to stay afloat; we just didn't have the money to pay creditors. I felt crippled when it came to dealing with the threatening messages on the voice mail from creditors, and we often left calls unreturned. We also noticed that our commitment to tithing weakened as we grew more and more frustrated in our predicament. Our bills kept piling up, and we were soon devastated and embarrassed by lawsuits and personal bankruptcy.

Since that time, we've learned that there are practical and positive steps to dealing with the financial rut:

1. *Pray for God's intervention*—not just for deliverance—and that He might teach you the lesson found in the "financial fire." Trust Him and remain faithful in your giving and sowing into God's work.
2. *The key to resolving financial conflict is in honest communication*—not in running away. Write a letter and set up a payment plan with creditors. We found that creditors just appreciated a wholehearted effort to make things right.

3. *Seek godly counsel and the wisdom from the Word.* The Book of Proverbs has excellent practical help in daily living for all of us. There are also excellent Christian resource books available that teach and encourage financial responsibility and accountability. Today, we have a board of qualified Christian businesspeople to help us in this critical area.

4. *We have made a deliberate point to keep credit cards out of our lives.* We also refuse to do any more projects on speculation. We have committed to moving forward only with God's provision.

5. *We ask God to identify covetousness in our lives.* Covetousness is a sin of desire that no one can see because it hangs on the coattails of ambition and success. It's the sin that turns a luxury into a necessity, robbing us of our contentment. (If you were to speak with any pastor, he would probably tell you that he has seen people come forward and confess practically every sin imaginable, but it's tough to find anyone confessing the sin of covetousness.)

If you have ever been in a financial crisis, you know the stress that can be put on your marriage and your family. Any unresolved financial issue can wipe your world away if you don't deal with it properly. If you owe someone money, whether it is a friend, family member, or creditor, don't ignore them. Learn how to deal with it. Let it be an opportunity to strengthen character and grow in wisdom.

· ·
Rest Stop

1. List any unresolved business or financial issues in your life.

2. In what way do you feel they have affected your relationships? Your emotional health?

3. What practical steps do you plan to take to resolve them? Make sure you and your husband are "one" in any decisions.

4. List some things that you have coveted. Can you identify why you are preoccupied with these things?

THE RUT OF PRIDE

Pride says, "I can handle this without You, God." It is the root of all disobedience and a source of great pain in our lives. When we walk in pride, we are separating ourselves from the very source of our strength, our hope—from our very life—because we are separating ourselves from God.

Often, we don't recognize pride because it is cleverly disguised as "self-love" and "self-confidence," not the self-worth that we have because we are made in the image of God and have been made worthy through Him. It is a confidence based on our own success and accomplishments—and continues only while we are succeeding or accomplishing, or as long as we are playing God.

When we place ourselves on the throne in our lives and reject the loving direction of our Creator, it always leads to destruction. (See Proverbs 16:18.) That is why God detests and opposes this behavior.

Lucifer spoiled the splendor of heaven when he decided in his heart that he didn't need God. And when he was expelled from heaven and banished to earth for a season, he used pride as the ultimate secret weapon to drive a wedge between the children of God and their Creator. The root of all pride is unbelief. To get out of this deep, deep rut we need to look truthfully at our need for God and at our own unworthiness apart from Him. Can we look in the mirror and say, "He is God, and I am not!"? Martin Luther said, "We are not loved by God because we are valuable; we are valuable because we are loved by God."

When we believe this, the pride in our lives begins to lose its stranglehold, and something stronger and far more beautiful begins to blossom and flourish in its place—the gentle strength of humility.

> The LORD detests all the proud of heart. Be sure of this: They will not go unpunished.
>
> —PROVERBS 16:5

....

Rest Stop

1. Write some examples of how pride has disrupted your life and your relationships.

2. Write a prayer of confession to God, asking His help in this area.

THE RUT OF HOLDING ON TO YOUR PAST

After you have looked at your hidden hurts—once you've learned the lessons from your past mistakes—it's time to let go. If you are unable to reflect on the past without bitterness, resentment, or anger, then that means you have not seen or understood how God wanted to let it teach you! God's Word says:

> Forget the former things; do not dwell on the past. See,

I am doing a new thing! . . . I am making a way in the desert and streams in the wasteland.

—Isaiah 43:18–19

When God brings you into the new way, and you've dealt with the pain in your life, it becomes a testimony—your personal story of what God has done in your life. The past, then, is only an illustration of our ways versus God's ways. When the pen is given back to the Author of your faith, the blood of Jesus blots out the crippling pain from the "old chapters" and with one majestic stroke begins a new story—a story of hope and victory.

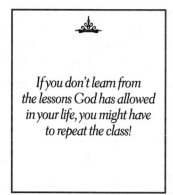

If you don't learn from the lessons God has allowed in your life, you might have to repeat the class!

When Shadrach, Meshach, and Abednego were brought out of the fiery furnace, they were not burned. In fact, they didn't even smell like smoke! If you and I are letting the "stink" of a fiery ordeal follow us around forever, then we have not experienced the victory of God's ways in the event! And when we continue to talk about it by pitying ourselves, or by bragging about our own "fire-walking" abilities, we are hurting ourselves and others. Let your past teach you, not torment you.

God causes everything to work together for the good of those who love God and are called according to his purpose for them.

—Romans 8:28, NLT

* *
Rest Stop

1. What specific issues or ordeals are still tormenting you?

2. Although the ordeal you've gone through may not have been the perfect will of God, is there a lesson God would like to teach you?

THE "I'LL-BE-HAPPY-WHEN . . ." RUT

Parents of every generation would probably agree that their ultimate wish for their children is happiness. "I just want you to be happy, dear." "Do whatever makes you happy, son." In my family, if happiness was the pot of gold at the end of every rainbow and the icing on every cake, then my dad was the grand marshal of the happiness parade! His family credo went *beyond* the realm of "happy." He wanted more. He wanted "instant happiness." He *demanded* it. And, superficial though it was, in some strange, demented, yet magical way, he often got it.

I remember one time when I was in high school, he was absolutely fed up with Susie (my stepmom) and me. Susie was so steaming mad at me that she hadn't thrown a word my direction all week. Dad, always wanting to get to the bottom of things, sat us down in the living room when he got home from work. "I'm sick of this!" he fumed. "I want instant happiness in this family!" His voice crescendoed as his face turned red and the veins in his neck bulged. "Now tell me why you two are acting like such brats, and then GET OVER IT!"

Susie wouldn't budge. I squealed, "Susie's mad at me 'cause I broke her crystal lamp. I said I was sorry, but she won't talk to me."

Susie's piercing glare said it all. I knew that the formal dining room was off-limits, and I knew that the crystal lamp was Susie's favorite. Sure, I felt bad for being careless and turning the lamp into a six-hundred-dollar pile of Austrian rubbish, but in my opinion a week of silent treatment and ice-cold stares was a bit too much. I returned Susie's glare with a snotty look of my own.

"I demand instant happiness!" My father insisted one last time. "Just get over it, you two!" Easier said than done. Susie was stone-faced, and I wasn't about to snap out of my bad mood. Could it be that "instant happiness" would elude the Goodman family this time? Not if my dad could help it. His fighter instinct kicked in. He was on a mission. As Susie and I stubbornly stormed out of the room, Dad immediately rolled up his sleeves and got to work.

As I was watching TV and Susie was stewing in the kitchen, Dad was methodically gathering up every single lamp in the house and exporting them into the backyard. Back and forth, in and out, up and down the staircase he trudged—unplugging every portable, luminous, electrical fixture from each room in the house and transporting them carefully into a sort of military formation on the grass in the backyard.

Susie, catching a glimpse of this strange parade, yelled from the kitchen, "Rosie, what is your father doing?" I peered out through the back window at the lunatic with the lamps. *He's really blown a fuse now,* I thought. A dozen lamps were standing at attention in my backyard, and my own father had banished them there. What cruel punishment awaited these poor, innocent victims? Just then, the mad leader of our household stormed in from the backyard and ordered us both out the back door. We complied out of sheer, morbid curiosity.

As we stood, confused and anxious, among the lamps, Dad suddenly pulled out two giant hammers from behind his back and brandished them heroically over his head. His booming voice echoed through the entire neighborhood. "I will never let lamps ruin my family or our happiness!"

The sheer spectacle of the scene had only just begun. My dad, the madman, thrust one of the giant hammers into my hands and the other one into Susie's. He then insisted that we utterly demolish the entire lamp population. I looked at my dad and then at the lamps. Slowly, I raised my weapon of destruction over my head with both fists. Before lowering the boom, I glanced over at Susie, whose jaw had dropped all the way to the grass. It was then—with hammer raised and innocent lamps cowering at my feet—that I suddenly burst into hysterical laughter. Then it was Susie's turn. She shook her head from side to side and smiled.

Dad wasn't satisfied with the broken mood. He wanted broken lamps. To him, these weren't innocent lamps at all. These old lamps would never again stop the Goodman family from being happy.

Susie and I smashed those lamps to smithereens. We laughed the whole time, and then, Dad took us both on a giant shopping spree for all new lamps—happy lamps!

Like my dad, many of us have fallen into the rut of the "I'll-be-happy-when..." syndrome. Think about it. It probably started when you were in school. When you were in high school you said, "I'll be happy when I'm a senior and I can rule the school." Then, when you were a senior, you said, "I'll be happy when I can move out of my parent's house and make my own rules." (At the time you didn't realize how blessed you were because you didn't have to pay any bills!) Then, when you moved out, you spent your single life saying, "I'll be happy when I'm married," because you didn't enjoy the time in your life when you weren't responsible for taking care of a household. (Imagine that!) Then after you got married, you may have said, "I'll be happy when the man I married changes so he can make me happy." Then, "I'll be happy when I have a baby." And the baby becomes a teenager, and it's, "I'll be happy when the baby moves out and I can have my life back." Unknowingly, you have fallen into the rut of "I'll be happy when . . . !"

What happens when you are always waiting for tomorrow? For the bigger house, nicer car, or better job? You will always wait and want for more. There is no "enough" apart from God. There is no "when" to the "I'll-be-happy . . ." syndrome.

In fact, it's not until you understand that your life's circumstances are not what brings you joy, but that your joy is found in walking through life with God—in spite of your cir-cumstances—that you will be truly happy.

Rest Stop

1. What blessings are in your life today that you are not enjoying because you are living in tomorrow?

2. List your blessings.

3. Thank God for your blessings by writing a prayer of thanksgiving.

4

Entering Into the Gates of Excellence

Living in excellence is a daily journey requiring discipline and hard work. Teddy Roosevelt said it best, "The victory only belongs to those who are actually in the arena of life." It's not achieved by sitting on the sidelines of life watching others—it's found in getting into the arena of life! If achieving excellence were easy, it would be a shallow victory.

You will find three types of people in this world. There are those who *watch* things happen, those who *make* things happen, and those who reach the end of their lives and sadly say, "What happened?" Make things happen in your life. Live on the Path of Excellence.

SEAL THE DELIVERANCE

As you receive emotional and spiritual healing on your journey, the next step is sealing the deliverance. When God brings you out of captivity, He wants you to learn how to live in the promised land. You are a new creation. You have a new way of living now. You don't need to look back any longer—rather, you can look forward to a hopeful future.

This is not the time to take things easy; rather it's the beginning of a more exciting walk with Him! Don't get distracted on this wonderful part of the journey! Protect yourself from slipping back into old patterns!

READ THE BIBLE

There are so many distractions competing for our time in today's society that it is easy to neglect the riches of truth found in the Scriptures. Becoming a student of the Word means we are intent on learning about God Himself—about His strength, His heart, His love, His grace, and His sacrifice. Use the Word to teach you how to live out God's call to excellence in your life. It is God's message of hope and healing to His children.

Basic Instructions Before Leaving Earth!

My son, pay attention to what I say; listen closely to my words. Do not let them out of your sight, keep them within your heart; for they are life to those that find them and health to a man's whole body.
—PROVERBS 4:20–22

Excellent people make excellent choices. Without the Word, we cannot obtain infinite wisdom. We've already wasted enough time trying to figure out how to live life on our own. It's time to stop doing things our way and do things the right way—which is God's way. Godly wisdom is the key to skillful living.

In other words, it's responding to life from God's perspective. One of the greatest places to start when seeking wisdom for everyday living is in the Books of Proverbs and

Ecclesiastes. These two books of the Bible were written by the wisest man who ever lived, King Solomon. Try to read a proverb each day and ask God to give you wisdom on how to apply it to your life.

....

Rest Stop

1. Do you find yourself sitting on the sidelines of life, or have you jumped into the arena?

2. In what areas of healing in your life do you need to "seal the deliverance"?

DON'T BE A LONE RANGER

Can you imagine if Christ had chosen only one disciple as He carried out His mission on earth? Just one. What if He left only one person to carry the message to the ends of the earth? But He didn't. He not only chose twelve, but He made friends everywhere He went!

The Christian walk was never meant to be taken alone. Don't try to be the "Lone Ranger" of the Christian faith. You need the accountability; you need the fellowship. You need the church! Attend a Bible-believing church. Get plugged into a weekly Bible study. Find people who know God's Word and will help you grow in Him.

....

Rest Stop

1. List a few Bible study or fellowship opportunities that you have been planning to explore. Set a goal and follow through with it.

Be Prepared for the Battle

As we walk on the Path of Excellence, we not only face battles with our human self, our flesh, but we also battle with spiritual forces. In Ephesians, Paul describes the spiritual battles that we face and warns us to put on the armor of God in order that we may stand strong against these powers.

> A final word: Be strong with the Lord's mighty power. Put on all of God's armor so that you will be able to stand firm against all strategies and tricks of the Devil. For we are not fighting against people made of flesh and blood, but against the evil rulers and authorities of the unseen world, against those mighty powers of darkness who rule this world, and against wicked spirits in the heavenly realm. Use every piece of God's armor to resist the enemy in the time of evil, so that after the battle you will be standing firm. Stand your ground, putting on the sturdy belt of truth and the body armor of God's righteousness. For shoes, put on the peace that comes from the Good News, so that you will be fully prepared. In every battle you will need faith as your shield to stop the fiery arrows aimed at you by Satan. Put on salvation as your helmet, and take the sword of the Spirit, which is the Word of God. Pray at all times and on every occasion in the power of the Holy Spirit. Stay alert and be persistent in your prayers for all Christians everywhere.
>
> —Ephesians 6:10–18, NLT

> For the word of God is living and active. Sharper than a double-edged sword . . .
>
> —Hebrews 4:12

We are in a real battle with real spiritual forces at work. Don't make the mistake of going into war unprepared.

....

Rest Stop

1. Write down examples of when the armor of God was a great help to you.

2. Now, write examples of when lacking the armor caused harm.

3. Turn Ephesians 6 into your own personal prayer:

Sᴇᴇᴋ Wɪsᴇ Cᴏᴜɴsᴇʟ

Be careful from whom you take advice! In order to live an excellent life, you will need to seek advice from excellent people. Be cautious when someone offers you free advice. Look at their life and look at their motives. Free advice, given by the wrong person, could end up costing you avoidable mistakes, misfortune, and misconduct. Remember, opinions are like belly buttons—everybody has one!

Luke 6:39 says, "What good is it for one blind person to lead another? The first will fall into a ditch and pull the other down also" (NLT).

I've learned this lesson the hard way. Usually, when someone is unhappy with life, it is natural for that person to say things that could cause you to stumble. Credibility is found in character.

Before you receive what could be a curse from someone, look at the character of the one delivering the word. I never seek advice from anyone I don't respect. We should observe a person's life from close range for a long time before that person gains our respect.

Blessed is the man [or woman] who does not walk in the counsel of the wicked or stand in the way of sinners or sit in the seat of mockers.

—PSALM 1:1

....
Rest Stop

1. Have you ever received advice that put you on the wrong road? Write about it in detail; also write what you learned from it.

2. List some people in your life whom you respect enough that you will take advice from them.

SURROUND YOURSELF WITH WHAT YOU WANT TO BECOME

Proverbs 13:20 says, "He who walks with the wise grows wise, but a companion of fools suffers harm."

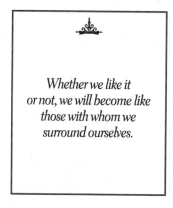

Whether we like it or not, we will become like those with whom we surround ourselves.

Your companions can be like buttons on an elevator—they can either take you up or bring you down. If we choose friends who are not living a life of excellence, we will begin to lower our standards. The key to staying strong and walking in excellence is in surrounding yourself with people who challenge and motivate you to be all that you can be!

....
Rest Stop

1. Make a list of people with whom you spend the most time.

2. Are these people lifting you up or bringing you down? Do you challenge each other to greatness or allow each other to feel comfortable with mediocrity?

FIND SOMEONE TO HOLD YOU ACCOUNTABLE

To keep your commitment to excellence, you will need to allow a special person to come into your world and, with your permission, hold you accountable. When selecting an accountability partner, consider the following:

- Does she know your heart?
- Does she know and understand your weaknesses?
- Does she have the same desire for excellence that you do?
- Are her motives pure?
- Does she live a life that you respect?

> Two people can accomplish more than twice as much as one; they get a better return for their labor. If one person falls, the other can reach out and help. . . . a triple-braided cord is not easily broken.
> —ECCLESIASTES 4:9–12, NLT

When two people stand together with God in the middle, they both will remain strong. Even Jesus sent His disciples out in twos. His Word promises that where two or more are gathered in His name, He is there in their midst. There will not be victory without accountability.

. . . .
Rest Stop

1. To whom do you go for advice?

2. Identify those with whom you've surrounded yourself. Are they having a positive or negative impact on your relationship with God?

3. Do they generally make you feel lost or as if you can't do anything right? Do they fail to give you practical advise that lasts?

CHOOSE YOUR BATTLES

Save your time and energy for the things worth fighting for—your children, godly values, marriage, purity, or health. Every day you're going to face some unexpected battles—long lines at the grocery store, a dirty house, bad hair, broken nails, or a rude dry-cleaning clerk. So examine each unexpected event in your schedule and figure out what kind of affect it is having on you. Then decide whether fighting a battle over it is worth losing your peace of mind and getting pushed out of "emotional shape."

Consider those around you. Have you thought about how your reactions to life's circumstances affect them? Remember, you can't always control what happens *to* you, but when it comes to the small stuff, you can control what happens *in* you! Life is not a dress rehearsal; you're not going to get another chance to make a positive difference in your world.

Rest Stop

1. List some battles you've been involved in that you now know you should have avoided.

2. When faced with an unexpected event in your life, what steps can you take to make sure you respond with wisdom (or, from God's perspective)?

GET THE FOCUS OFF YOURSELF

What do you want to be when you grow up in God? Or, better yet, what does God want you to be when you grow up in Him? It was twenty years ago when my English teacher in high school told me I'd never amount to anything if I continued down the path of destruction on which I was walking. It was at that point that I made my first plan to clean up my life: *I acknowledged my own need to change, and I began the process.*

Excuses are the nails that build a house of failure.

After I overcame my drug and food addictions and went through an emotional healing, I was anxious to make a difference in the lives of others, but I didn't know how to start. Up to this point I had only focused on myself and all the obstacles that surrounded me. I knew it was time to make a new plan. A plan that would benefit not just me, but would contribute to society. There comes a point when you have to stop focusing on your own problems, leave your pity party, and stop making excuses! One of the greatest ways to experience fulfillment is using your life to touch another's. When you use your passion for the purpose of benefiting others, you experience the true joy of living.

Rest Stop

1. If we don't write out our dreams and goals on

paper, we will continue to wander aimlessly through life. There's nothing worse than not knowing where you are going and killing yourself to get there. Write out your goals, your passions, and your dreams. Everyone has to start somewhere, so start now.

2. Where do you want to be five to ten years from now?

3. What can you do to take the first step to get there?

CONTRIBUTE TO OTHERS

One of the greatest ways to seal a deliverance after receiving healing is to get our focus off ourselves and on something productive and meaningful. Think about volunteering two times a month for a nonprofit organization that touches your heart. Take up a new activity like tennis, rollerblading, art, or drama. Be in a play. There are many community options that you can do to make a difference in society.

The goal is to provide ourselves with opportunities to share our victories with others. Whatever it is you decide to do, do it well. Do it unselfishly. Do it to make a positive dent in society. We may not be able to change the entire world, but we can change the world for just one person.

There was a little boy walking on a beach in the middle of thousands upon thousands of starfish that had washed up on shore. Seeing their deadly predicament, he began picking them up one at a time and throwing them back into the water. An old man who happened along saw what the young boy was doing and laughed, "You'll never be able to save all those starfish, young man!" The little boy looked up at the man and then across the sea of starfish that lay dying before him. He then bent over and picked up another starfish, threw it into the ocean, and said, "Maybe I can't save them all, but I saved that one."

Any contribution you make to society, no matter how small it seems to you, can make a significant difference in someone's life. Even by setting a good example for others to follow, we can be a positive influence on someone's journey through life.

My husband and I live in an apartment complex that is filled with young boys without daddies. My husband wanted to do something to make an impact on these boys' lives. He decided that he would start going out to the park with them three times a week to play football. Even though he will never be able to meet their need for a father, the few hours he spends investing in their lives is making a difference. He was able to experience the joy of his giving when one of the single moms came to our door with tears of gratitude to thank my husband for helping her son to believe in himself again.

·····························
Rest Stop

1. Write out how you can use your passion for the purpose of blessing someone else.

2. Seal it in prayer. Write out a prayer of your passions and plans to God and watch what happens!

Be prepared for adverse reactions! With each victory in my life, I've experienced many adverse reactions. When I stopped using drugs, the kids at school stopped inviting me to parties. When I lost weight, my girlfriends became jealous and didn't want to hang around with me anymore, and my guy friends refused to go out with me unless I would sleep with them. When I became a Christian, my Jewish family didn't want anything to do with me. When God gave me a platform for ministry, people began to judge me harshly. When I won the crown of Mrs. USA, women started to treat me as though I were a plastic Barbie with a Bible. Throughout my life, I have experienced loneliness and isolation. At times I have been so discouraged that I've wondered if it would be easier to *not* excel in life—perhaps then I would be more loved and accepted.

If you are going to be all that God created you to be and walk on the Path of Excellence, you will have to make a choice—are you going to please man, or are you going to please God?

When you walk on the Path of Excellence, you are likely to notice adverse reactions from those around you. Often, people will either respect you or resent you. They can join you, ignore you, or leave you. They can share in your passion or they can cause you pain. They can follow your example and better themselves, or they can grow bitter towards you.

Certainly someone's insensitive attitude and sinful behavior will stir some unpleasant or negative emotions within you. Be encouraged by identifying your emotions with Christ and the suffering and emotional pain He endured. Those who choose to take the Path of Excellence don't let others keep them down—they allow God to lift them up. God promises, "When a man's ways are pleasing to the LORD, he makes even his enemies live at peace with him" (Prov. 16:7).

··························
Rest Stop

1. Are you currently experiencing any "adverse reactions" from others around you?

2. Write a prayer asking for God's help and comfort in this difficult and painful area.

SET BOUNDARIES

As you are sealing the deliverance in your life, it is very important to set boundaries—especially in our distracting and overstimulating culture. Picture "boundaries" as a fence around you and your family. *What* and *who* are you going to allow into that precious, private place of refuge and protection?

- What television programs will you watch?
- What movies will you see?
- What kind of music will fill the air in your home and in your car?
- How much time will you spend talking on the phone today, and with whom will it be?
- What will be the purpose of your conversations, and how will you spend your time?
- Of what will your quiet time consist, if anything?
- How much of life's demands will you pursue?
- How valuable is your time? Your husband's time? Your kids?

To seal the deliverance in our lives, it's important that we protect ourselves and what is important to us. That is what boundaries are all about. For instance, my time is so valuable to me that I would never stay on the phone with someone who is yelling or verbally abusive. I also unplug my phone after 8:00 P.M. every night so I can have special time with my son. When I'm talking to people, I've also learned to recognize gossip and ungodly conversations as not only dangerous poison to any relationship, but also huge time-wasters. I just can't afford it.

Our family makes a point to not watch TV shows or movies that don't match our value system. Once, not too long ago, I convinced my husband to go to a movie on our date night that looked like it might be really funny. Neither of us had heard that much about it, so we went. We were so turned off by the story and the characters that, halfway through the movie, we stood up in the middle of the theater and walked out. Some people looked at us like we were a couple of old-fashioned prudes trying to make some kind of right-wing point. *The truth is, our time is precious; we were trying to be good stewards of our time by protecting our boundaries.*

....

Rest Stop

1. Let's get specific. In what areas in your life do you feel a need to be protected?

2. Can you detect any unwise distractions that have invaded that valuable area in your life?

3. What boundaries do you think you should set up to protect these areas?

PREVENT DISTRACTIONS

I have learned that our *daily routine* determines our *future success!* Many of us are extremely busy, yet unproductive and distracted. Remember, if the devil can't make you bad, his next trick is to make you busy! Look at your daily routine and ask yourself the following questions:

1. What are your priorities? Does this schedule match your priorities?

2. Will this routine get you where you want to be five, ten, or twenty years from now? Is it bringing order to your days and peace to your mind?

3. Is there anything that can be edited out of your daily routine that would give you more time to rest, reflect, exercise, and pursue your goals?

I only have four priorities in my life, and my daily routine revolves around them:

- My relationship with God
- My time with my family
- The Fit for Excellence Program
- My health and taking care of God's temple

I've learned that if the devil can't defeat you, he will try to distract you daily so you will become discouraged! He is the author of confusion and chaos, but God is the God of order. Write out an order to your day first thing each morning to keep you from getting distracted or discouraged.

Rest Stop

Take a moment to write out a sample of your typical daily routine, including phone, work, people, TV shows, etc.

Morning:

Late Morning:

Noon Time:

Afternoon:

Evening:

Late Night:

Now write out your dream schedule as if there were no obstacles in the way. Write it down without any restrictions:

Morning:

Late Morning:

Noon Time:

Afternoon:

Evening:

Late Night:

Now write out what unnecessary things in your daily routine are stopping you from living out your dream routine (TV, telephone, unproductive relationships, too many commitments):

Morning:

Late Morning:

Noon Time:

Afternoon:

Evening:

Late Night:

Pray and ask God for wisdom in planning out your daily routine. In order for you to walk in excellence every day, start your day with prayer. Once you have prayed, write out a realistic routine that has all unproductive and distracting things edited out of it.

Morning:

Late Morning:

Noon Time:

Afternoon:

Evening:

Late Night:

Take a moment to write out this schedule on a separate piece of paper; place one copy on your bathroom mirror and one copy in your daily planner. (If you don't have a daily planner, get one!)

●

5

Climb That Mountain

Overcoming Obsession With Food

The Path of Excellence is not always easy. For many of us, even after we've heeded the warning signs and made it out of the ruts of emotional pain, we still have more to conquer! There is a huge mountain in front of us, and we are stuck *right where we are until we can climb it.* "It" is the mountainous problem of food addiction!

For years I have been sharing my personal testimony, yet trying to avoid the subject of food and weight loss out of fear that it might offend people. But every time I shared how I broke the bondage of bulimia, conquered chronic fatigue, lost over fifty pounds, and kept it off, women would bombard me with questions on how.

Not long ago, I read an article in a Christian magazine that said a recent survey of churches in America revealed that 90 percent of all prayer requests involved a need for physical healing. After reading that article, I decided to offer a physically "Fit for Excellence" workshop at a women's retreat where I was scheduled to speak. I planned on addressing the issues of overeating, exhaustion, and food addiction. I was overwhelmed by the response. Of the fifteen hundred women attending the retreat, thirteen hundred of them came to my workshop. Women everywhere are wanting help.

"I'M SO-O-O-O FAT!"

I've discovered that whenever you ask a woman how she is doing, you will probably get one of four answers: "I'm so tired!" "I'm so bloated!" "I'm so sick!" Or, "I'm so-o-o-o fat!" Then we get together in a group while we're pigging out on cakes, candy, coffee, and chips, and talk on and on about how sick, tired, and fat we are! What is wrong with this picture?

After trashing our bodies, we drop to our knees, bow our heads, and beg God to help us not to feel sick! We know that we need healing and that God can heal us, but we make His temple our trash can! It's like drinking a bottle of whiskey before coming to church and praying to God to help us not feel drunk!

Honestly, the reason I can talk so freely about this subject is because, well, I am a *food addict!* The only thing I love doing more than talking is eating! One of my greatest joys in life is food. When I'm celebrating, I eat. When I'm tired, I eat. When I'm sad, I eat. When I'm anxious, I eat. When I'm in pain, I eat. I have spent years running to the refrigerator for refuge. And when I get hungry, my personality actually changes— from Dr. Jekyll to Mr. Hyde! While others may snack off-and-on all day long, I actually prefer eating only one meal a day—it starts in the morning and ends when I fall asleep!

In the past, when at a restaurant, I used to eat until I was completely bloated and then tackle the waiter for the dessert menu! When weddings took too long, I would get irritated because I couldn't wait to get to the reception to eat. I've been known to push people out of line so I could get the corner piece of cake that has the most icing! Of all the obstacles in my life, my addiction to food has been the most difficult for me to overcome. In fact, I even came up with three good reasons *not* to control my eating habits:

1. *The chocolate industry might go broke.*
2. *We need to support the companies that make control pantyhose.*
3. *What would I talk about if I felt good?* Being bloated, sick, and tired are very popular topics of conversation.

TAKING RESPONSIBILITY

Seriously, most of us do have many "reasons" for not taking responsibility for our eating habits:

1. *I'm too busy to prepare healthy food or to exercise.*
2. *It's too hard, and I don't have the will power.*
3. *We live in a toxic world anyway, so why waste my time trying to be healthy?*
4. *I'll offend people if I don't eat junk food.* (Everybody else eats it.)
5. *The quicker I die, the quicker I get to heaven.*
6. *It really doesn't matter what I eat.*

Here are the results of our good reasons. It's time to face the facts.

- FACT: One out of three of us will develop cancer in our lifetime.
- FACT: Five hundred thousand a year die from cancer.
- FACT: One million will die from heart disease this year.
- FACT: Two out of three Americans are overweight.
- FACT: An alarming number of Americans suffer from chronic fatigue.

- FACT: Millions more suffer from severe depression because they're too exhausted to handle the daily pressures of life.

> Don't you know that you yourselves are God's temple and that God's Spirit lives in you? If anyone destroys God's temple, God will destroy him; for God's temple is sacred, and you are that temple.
> —1 CORINTHIANS 3:16–17

Isn't it interesting that the first fall of man had to do with disobedience over food? Adam and Eve saw that the fruit from the forbidden tree was pleasing to the eye, good for food, and able to make them wise, so they ate. The devil still uses that same trick on us today. Many things are pleasing to the eye and good for food, but remember, the devil comes to steal, kill, and destroy; as long as we make God's temple our trash can, the devil can accomplish his mission—one meal at a time.

Our bodies are *the physical vessel* that God uses while we're here on earth; we need to take care of it in honor of Him. Jesus Himself borrowed an earthly body while He was here on earth, and He wants to use you to accomplish even greater things! (See John 1:14.)

Dream with me for a minute. If all of us took care of our bodies for the right reasons, the right way—through proper nutrition, exercise, and rest—the results would be amazing:

1. *Imagine our pastors, evangelists, and missionaries having the health and energy to finish their ministries strong.* Studies show that only one out of ten pastors will still be in the ministry by the time they reach sixty years of age—physical and emotional burn-out being the major cause.
2. *Think about how much money would be saved on medical bills and health insurance.*

A friend of mine recently interviewed with a national Fortune 500 pharmaceutical company. She happened to have some literature from the Fit for Excellence program and showed it to one of the executives from the company. He took one look at it and tossed it down with a smirk, "This program better not work, or we'll go broke! We make millions off of women who are overweight, depressed, and tired!"

3. *If we invest in ourselves now, we'll be able to enjoy the wisdom that comes with age and the treasures of grandchildren.* Think about how many wonderful older people are too sick or too tired to enjoy the golden years of their life.
4. *Members would have more energy for outreach programs and special ministries* if our churches started encouraging good nutrition and a healthy lifestyle.

When you think about it, Christians *should* be the healthiest, happiest people on earth! After all, we know where we're going. We have life's instruction manual (the Bible), and we serve a God who has shown us, through His Word, how to take care of His temple—our bodies. But only if we take the necessary steps to be healthy will we be able to enjoy the abundance God promises.

THE "G" WORD

Does God really care how much we eat? That question is clearly answered in Proverbs. "When you sit to dine . . . note well what is before you, and put a knife to your throat if you are given to gluttony" (Prov. 23:1–2). Let's face it—overeating is gluttony! And gluttony is sin!

This scripture is a hard one for me to swallow, because I love tasty food no matter how bad it is for my body. My biggest weakness, however, is healthy snacks. You leave me alone in a health food store and . . . watch out! I could justify pigging out on excessive calories and fat grams all day long if the food is labeled "organic," "natural," or "fresh-baked." I've been known to eat two dozen "healthy" cookies in one sitting! I tell people, "At least my cellulite is organic!"

When you think about it, though, none of us feel good after we've stuffed ourselves, do we? We feel guilty, we feel tired, and we feel angry at ourselves for our lack of self-control. Our stomachs were designed with a built-in gauge. First comes *E* for empty, then comes *F* for full. Unfortunately, we don't always stop at *F*; we go straight to *G* for glutton! *G* also stands for guilt, and this guilt was placed there by God as a warning sign. We should not ignore it!

Unfortunately, many of us would rather figure out a way to get rid of our guilt than deal with our problem of overeating. Overeating seems to be the one "acceptable sin." And because everybody does it, it's easier to ignore. Don't ignore it.

DISCIPLINE

I'm often inspired by the discipline of the prophet Daniel and his friends. They were willing to give up eating the delicious food prepared at the king's palace and eat God's diet because they were committed to not defiling their bodies—God's temple. Because of their obedience, God blessed them with extra knowledge, extra favor, and extra strength. In fact, in matters of wisdom and understanding, the king found that Daniel and his friends were ten times better than their peers. (See Daniel 1.)

Another example of discipline is Esther. She spent a whole *year* preparing to compete for the hand of the king in a royal beauty pageant! Do you think if she had stuffed her face that she'd be wearing those royal robes? She made it a priority to take care of herself, and God blessed her with incredible favor and even used her to save her people.

A NEW WAY OF THINKING

Our diet is not about *denial;* it's about *desire!* Do you think you can live your dreams and accomplish your goals if you don't feel good about yourself? I know from experience how hard it is to receive the truth of this message. I've found that it really takes a renewing of my mind, a new way of thinking.

> Therefore, I urge you, brothers, in view of God's mercy, to offer your bodies as living sacrifices, holy and pleasing to God—this is your spiritual act of worship. Do not conform any longer to the pattern of this world, but be transformed by the renewing of your mind.
>
> —ROMANS 12:1–2

Isn't it interesting that when the Bible talks about offering sacrifices to God, our bodies are the only sacrifice that must be presented "living"? Being changed by renewing our mind means to see things from God's point of view, and that includes a godly view of our physical bodies and how we should take care of these "living sacrifices."

BREAKING THE ADDICTION

There is no easy way to break a food addiction. You can't do it alone! You must find someone to hold you accountable and pray you through. This and the following chapters will give you the plan and steps that I used to break my addiction to food and lose over fifty pounds! It's not a quick weight-loss gimmick, it's not a diet pill, it's not a secret formula—*it's a way of life.* You can be all that God has called you to be. You were created in God's image; therefore, your image is important to God.

Two major points that will give you strength to stick to this plan are:

1. *Accountability*
2. *A steady diet of "spiritual" food—prayer and the Word of God* (Without the emotional healing and spiritual deliverance that I experienced, I would never have been able to break out of this addiction!)

The following are practical steps to help set you free and keep you free from addiction to food. Keep in mind that these are some ideas that I have found to work for me; they are not intended to replace the advice of a health professional!

Steps to Success

Step 1: Confession

The first step to my deliverance from food addiction was when I understood that overeating is a sin and that I needed to ask God to forgive me for hurting my body. I also understood that the reason I felt guilty was because I was! Food is a gift from God to enjoy, but when we overindulge, we are abusing this gift.

Step 2: Identify

You must identify the root problems of your food addiction! I learned that my overeating was due to a much deeper issue than my love for food. In fact, there were many unresolved issues in my life. I worried constantly about the future and lived in my past. It wasn't until I identified my problems and dealt with them that I was able to break my addiction to food.

Step 3: Prayer

I know that overeating is a weakness that I cannot stop on my own. God's Word says that if we ask, the Lord will be strong in our weakness. I begin each morning asking God for the strength to avoid overeating. When I recognized that my weakness was a spiritual issue, it was easier to hand over control to God.

Step 4: Accountability

After I identified the root of my problem, I found an accountability partner with the same goals. We called each other each morning to pray and encourage one another to eat the right foods and not to overeat. We also exercised or walked together at least three times a week. (If you are looking for an accountability partner, my suggestion is that you select a friend, not your spouse.)

Step 5: Censor!

Because of my love for food and my tendency to overeat, I make an effort not to bring foods into my home that will be tempting. Just as an alcoholic breaking an addiction doesn't stock his cabinets with alcoholic beverages, I don't stock my cabinets with tempting food and then try in my own strength not to eat! At first, these changes were a little hard on my family because they loved junk food as much as I did. But I was honest with them about my addiction, and they agreed to help me by not bringing tempting foods home. Besides, they know that "if Mom isn't happy—no one's happy!"

Step 6: Move Your Body

I try to exercise at least twenty to thirty minutes a day. Because of my need for constant change, sometimes I walk with a friend, sometimes I swim, sometimes I go to a gym, and sometimes I use an exercise video or my home exercise equipment. When I'm really bored, I blare my Christian music and dance in the living room with my dog.

There are so many creative ways to move your body! You can park twenty minutes from where you work, you can hike (or play tag) with your children, you can run up and down the stairs in your house, you can race your shopping cart through the supermarket, or you can walk really fast through the mall (this is also good for your budget!). Whatever you do, it's important that you DO IT! Your body will be blessed.

Step 7: Prepare

Like most women today, I have a very busy schedule. It's challenging to make time to prepare the proper foods and resist the fast-food drive-thrus—called "fast food" because it's better to fast than to eat the food! However, preparing in advance is essential. Try these preparation tips:

- Pick one day a week and do all your preparations at once.
- Cut up raw vegetables and put them in plastic bags. I wash my lettuce, dry it thoroughly with paper towels, and store it in plastic bags.
- Cut up fresh fruit and soak in lemon juice.
- Boil six to eight hormone-free eggs for quick protein snacks or to use in salads.
- Make two dozen of my "Make-over Muffins" (see recipe at end of chapter).
- Steam four to six cups of brown rice and store in plastic ware in the refrigerator. I use brown rice for stir-fry with vegetables and chicken breast or plain with a meal.
- Boil four to six chicken breasts (hormone-free), then let them cool, dice them up, and store in plastic bags in the refrigerator. These are used in salads and for stir-fry.
- Take two cups of nonfat yogurt, mix with any favorite seasoning, and use for veggie dip.

- Make a gallon of decaffeinated, fruit-flavored iced tea and add fruit juice and fresh lemons. Store in the refrigerator for a refreshing drink.
- Make sure that there is a big bowl of fresh fruit set out on a table.
- Place two quarts of distilled water in the refrigerator each morning, and make a goal to finish it off before going to bed.

Step 8: Shop to Drop . . . Pounds

I try never to shop when I'm hungry because I always end up buying foods that make me fat. I do best if I make a list before I go. See my sample shopping list at the end of the chapter.

Step 9: Change Mind-Set

Don't think of your diet as a denial, but rather as a desire to be fit for God! Think about the great things you will be able to do if you remain healthy and feel good about yourself!

I know from personal experience that God rewards obedience. His reward is worth the sacrifice of the unhealthy foods you love to eat. Taking care of God's temple is my responsibility and one of the ways of showing God that I love Him.

Step 10: Stop

Try to stop eating after 7:00 P.M. I find that I sleep better if I'm not full, and I wake up with more energy. If I break the late-night snack rule, it's usually with raw fruits or raw vegetables because they are more easily digested. When I go to bed stuffed, my poor body has to work well into the night to digest everything I swallowed. Without fail, I wake up bloated and exhausted and have trouble finding the energy to roll out of bed.

Step 11: Control

List on your refrigerator all of the benefits of being thin and healthy. When you are tempted to overeat, the list will help you overcome your obsession with food. Also, I find I can keep myself from overeating if I eat my food off a salad plate. Salad plates are smaller, and I can still "fill it up" and not worry about being a pig.

Step 12: Reward

When I stick to my plan for the day, I reward myself with something fun or relaxing that I really enjoy like a bubble bath, renting a good movie, making a fire in the fireplace, or talking on the phone with a girlfriend for an hour.

MORE TIPS

Caution about carbohydrates: Most people eat far too many carbohydrates. When I need to lose weight, I stop eating flour and sugar completely. Even while I am maintaining, I eat very little bread, pasta, and fruit. Too much will end up being stored as fat, so try to keep a good balance with each meal between proteins, complex carbohydrates (brown rice, beans, etc.), and vegetables. If you overdo the carbs, your blood sugar will go up and your energy will sink in a matter of minutes.

Eating out: Because of my travel schedule, I am forced to eat out quite often. I'd have to say that going to restaurants is one of my biggest joys—and one of my greatest challenges.

First of all, it is hard to find healthy food, and, at most restaurants, the portions have "glutton" written all over them! (My husband and I almost always share a meal.)

Secondly, I love trying new foods. When I'm at a restaurant, the last thing I want to do is eat the same foods I have at home. Because I can only eat a limited amount of carbohydrates, I either eat the bread, the potato, or the dessert, but I rarely eat all three in one meal. If I decide to eat a dessert, I ask the waiter not to bring bread to the table.

One of the biggest culprits when dining out is a soda. I never drink anything with my meal except water or mineral water. Why waste my calories—and money—on a sugary beverage? You'll find that once you cut out the sodas, you will soon prefer water. By following these few simple suggestions, I've found that I can avoid gaining weight while eating out.

Emotions: It is important to understand the connection between our emotions and our physical health. In Pam Smith's book *Food For Life,* she cites some important research that shows stress-related emotions can have a profound negative affect on our health. Unprocessed emotions—particularly negative ones like bitterness, anger, resentment, and general irritability—"may increase production of certain hormones that are responsible for reducing the body's ability to fight disease."[1]

In addition, researchers have known for years that emotions like anxiety and fear have a significant negative affect on the digestive system. Recognize the major connection between your emotional health and your physical health and deal with yourself as a whole person.

Blowing it: If you do blow it at one meal, one of the worst things you can do is condemn yourself over and over again. Make a point not to stress out about it; just get back on track at the next meal, doing it the right way.

Negative attitudes: When you feel negative attitudes surfacing, do your best to get your focus back on health for godly reasons. Self-defeating behavior says, "My body and my health are not important!"

Remember it's worth it! The time and energy it takes to eat healthy and exercise is well worth every minute. Be strong in the Lord's strength, do your very best, and God will do the rest.

1. If you're an overeater, list as many reasons as you can for overeating.

2. Look back over this list and see if you recognize which reasons are emotional, which are physical, and which are spiritual. Make comments below.

3. If you are like I was, and you can't stop over-eating on your own, write out a prayer to God, asking Him to forgive you and give you the strength to take care of His temple, your body.

4. List one or two people who you feel would be good accountability partners for you in your quest to be fit for excellence.

5. From what you have learned in this chapter, write out the steps that you can realistically apply to your daily routine.

Fit for Excellence

Recipe: Make-over Muffins

Ingredients:

4 cups oat bran
2 fertile eggs
2 cups rice milk
$\frac{1}{2}$ cup pure maple syrup
1 Tbsp. baking powder
1 Tbsp. canola oil
$\frac{1}{2}$ cup raw slivered almonds

Preheat oven to 400 degrees. Combine ingredients together. Bake for 15–17 minutes. Once cool, store in baggies and freeze. Warm up as needed in microwave.

Sheri's Shopping List

- raw vegetables
- raw fruit
- raw nuts
- brown rice
- rice cakes
- eggs (hormone-free)
- whole-grain bread
- oat bran
- oatmeal
- herbal tea
- distilled water
- green barley powder
- sliced turkey
- rice milk
- chicken breast (hormone-free)
- no-salt tuna
- salad dressing (not diet)

1. Pamela M. Smith, R.D., *Food For Life* (Lake Mary, FL: Creation House, 1997), 130.

6

Deactivating Land Mines

Uncovering Eating Disorders

Consider the following questions:

- Do you compulsively eat massive amounts of food when you're in emotional pain?
- Do you exercise so excessively that you harm your body?
- Do you weigh yourself excessively (more than once a day)?
- Is every meal a mental battle?
- Do you take laxatives or diuretics to lost weight?
- Do you starve yourself to get thin?
- Do you throw up your food?
- Do you feel completely out of control of your eating habits?

If you've answered *yes* to any of the above questions, let me assure you, you're not alone. Over eight million women in America battle with an eating disorder, a private prison that only God Himself can unlock the cell door and set us free.

Needless to say, eating disorders are land mines on the Path of Excellence. The path may be smooth and quiet for a while, but left untreated and with a little pressure added, an explosion *will* occur. An explosion that can create havoc in your health—and maybe even kill you.

ANOREXIA

Anorexia is a life-threatening problem with serious medical consequences—heart problems, liver and kidney damage, and nervous system damage. The anorexic is often very secretive about her behaviors. She may try to dress in baggy clothes to disguise the weight loss.

BULIMIA

Bulimia is a binge-and-purge syndrome. Unlike anorexia, people with bulimia are usually at a normal weight or even slightly overweight. They may be able to hide the disorder for several years, knowing that they have a problem, but feeling a great deal of shame and hiding it. I know . . . I've felt that shame.

When I first set out to lose my weight as a teenager, my stepmom Susie taught me how to eat healthy, take care of my body, and exercise moderately. By following her instructions, I lost all my extra weight, regained my health and energy, and enjoyed the benefits of a healthy lifestyle for almost four years.

It wasn't until I was sitting at a modeling audition watching three beautiful, thin, young girls eating several candy bars at a time that my problems began. As I sat there and watched these three young ladies obviously enjoying themselves, it drove me crazy. I couldn't stand not knowing. "How can you possibly eat all that candy and stay so thin?" I blurted out.

They looked back at me as they fumbled with handfuls of wrappers—their cheeks so stuffed they could hardly speak.

"Easy," they mumbled. "We just go to the bathroom and throw it up!"

Ooooh, yuck! I thought to myself. *How disgusting!*

A few weeks later, I made the mistake of stuffing myself at a dinner. Afterward, a strange fear gripped me as an old familiar thought popped into my head, *Sheri Rose, look what you did! You just ate like a pig, and now you're going to be fat again!*

That fear gave me the impulse to go to the bathroom and try something that, just a few days before, was unthinkable. *After all, those beautiful, thin models did it,* I thought. *Just this once . . . I've got to get this food out of my body!* I had no idea that "just that once" was going to turn into a life-threatening habit.

From that day on, every meal became a mental battle—a desperate, private struggle between my desire to be thin and the pleasure of eating. *Should I eat right, or should I eat what I want and just throw it up?*

As I entered into this bulimic lifestyle, I learned there were other tricks to control my weight. I began using laxatives and water pills and exercised compulsively. I hopped nervously onto the scale at least five times a day to make sure I wasn't putting on any extra pounds. I was so obsessed with my body that I couldn't concentrate on any other area of my life.

I knew I was in bondage, but I was afraid to tell anybody what I was doing to myself, fearful that others would see me as a failure. I tried with all my strength and will power to control my unhealthy, compulsive-eating behavior, but the harder I tried to break out of this bondage, the more bound I became.

I felt as if I were doomed to be locked up forever in this private prison. People gladly accepted me outwardly, but, behind closed doors, I was a total failure. What started out as a quick and easy weight-loss strategy ended up rotting my teeth, damaging my kidneys, and weakening my heart. Every part of my body suffered pain in this disastrous personal hell. Of all the poor choices I have ever made, this has been the one I regret the most. It's embarrassing, it's scary, it's lonely, and it's hard to find help. It's a private sin from which only God Himself can deliver you.

Gratefully, God has healed me of this terrible eating disorder. But once you have opened the door to sin, it can tempt you again. I used to think that once I prayed for God to heal me, I would never have to battle with bulimia again. I've grown up a lot since then.

Paul, in his letter to the church in Rome, describes the battle between the flesh and the spirit within us. While we may have every intention of doing the right thing, sometimes we fall prisoner to the sinful nature within us. Paul cried out to be rescued from this bondage and found that Jesus Christ was there to rescue him without condemning him. (See Romans 7–8.)

WALKING IN THE SPIRIT

God freed me from the bondage of bulimia. But the key to my deliverance from bulimia was not just in a prayer, but also *in taking the necessary steps to walk in the Spirit and seal the deliverance!* When God delivers you out of bondage, He always directs you somewhere better!

By the time the Israelites were delivered out of Egypt, they had grown so accustomed to the feeling of bondage and slavery that when God set them free, it felt foreign to them. They didn't know how to handle it. They soon lost sight of their goal—the Promised Land—and started grumbling.

I've found that there are many things I have had to change in my life to *remain free*. The following are the practical steps that God used in my life. These are my personal steps and are not intended to take the place of professional medical advice!

And remember, without the emotional healing and spiritual deliverance that I had experienced also, I would not have victory today.

Steps to Freedom

Step 1: Confess

When I first learned that bulimia was not only destroying my body but was also destroying God's temple, it was hard for me to confess that I was in sin—I could not have stopped even if I had wanted to stop. Today, I know that when I confess my sin, He is faithful to forgive me and make me as white as snow (1 John 1:9). When the bulimic thoughts come, I immediately confess them to God.

Step 2: Identify

My next step to freedom was in identifying the root problem that caused my compulsive eating behavior. Unveiling the hidden hurts in your life will show you how God's power will help break the bondage of eating disorders.

Step 3: Power of Prayer

When I have the urge to purge, I no longer hide it or try to handle it by myself. I've learned there is power in numbers, so I go to someone I trust who knows how to pray. I then ask that person to pray me through the temptation. The devil would love for you to try to deal with this by yourself. The Word of God says, "Where two or three are gathered together in my name, there am I in the midst of them" (Matt. 18:20, KJV). If you do not have someone in your life to pray with, ask God to send you someone or call a local Bible-believing church right away. You can ask them to direct you to a church that has an eating disorder prayer support group.

Step 4: Don't Compare

One of the more popular pastimes these days is comparing

ourselves to other people. I grew up constantly comparing my body to those of models and movie stars. If we're not careful, this can lead to ungratefulness, insecurity, and eventually the sin of covetousness. God made each one of us unique and special; we need to look to His face for our mirror.

Step 5: Throw Out the Scale

It's hard to believe a little pressure-sensitive device that lived on the floor in my bathroom could have the power to absolutely, utterly destroy my day. My scale truly became an idol to me. Some people bow down to their idols, others drive them to work, while still others set them in front of their sofa and stare at them. I stepped on my idol five times a day. Today, I no longer worry about my weight. I've thrown out my scale, and I've changed my focus from my weight to my health.

Remember, if you wander aimlessly like the Israelites did, you're bound to end up longing for the security of your old chains. Eventually you'll end up back in the prison where you started. When I stray and try to handle my eating disorder in my own strength, not sticking to the program that God revealed to me, I return to the prison from which God had set me free.

There is no easy answer. There can be no victory unless there is a battle. You will have to fight for your freedom. Depend on God's strength, not your own, to win this war. An eating disorder is not only a battle of the flesh, but a battle of the mind and of the Spirit!

••••••••••••••••••••••••••••
Rest Stop

1. Have you recognized any of the symptoms of an eating disorder in your own life? If so, which ones?

2. Are any of these symptoms seriously affecting your health at this time? If so, list one or two trusted friends who will help you to receive treatment.

3. If you are not currently dealing with an eating disorder, do you see yourself in some of the symptoms listed? What are some precautions that you can take now to avoid this in your future?

Make sure to look at the root problem causing the eating disorder. Remember: If you don't deal with your pain, it will deal with you.

As you begin to deactivate this land mine in your life, be patient with yourself. If you have a day when you fall back into the prison cell, remember *you have the keys to get back out.* Do your best to allow God to do the rest. Most importantly, don't fight this battle alone!

7

Swimming Upstream

Fighting Exhaustion

Do you feel that instead of walking on the Path of Excellence you're swimming upstream? Are you trapped in an exhausted body and just can't seem to get out? Or are you one of those people who can eat whatever you want, whenever you want, get very little sleep, and have bundles of extra energy to spare? (If so, then this chapter is definitely not for you!)

I used to travel through life in two gears: park and fifth. I managed to strip all the others. I would push myself past the highest speed limits known to man, ignoring the big yellow warning lights screaming, "Slow down! Stop! Rest! Severe exhaustion ahead!" I was so consumed with getting to my destination of the day that I was living life in fast forward. And just when I didn't think I could handle traveling one more mile, I pushed myself and added two. I thought the scripture that said, "The Spirit is willing, but the flesh is weak," meant that it's not spiritual to rest, relax, or restore your body. I was convinced that every opportunity to do the work of the Lord must belong to me—even if I wasn't called or equipped to do it! I found myself saying *yes* to any and every opportunity that seemed like a good cause. Needless to say, I did not respect my humanity.

Finally, my compulsive behavior took over. But I didn't recognize it as a compulsive-behavior problem because I loved everything I was doing. I was helping people and felt like I was accomplishing something significant with my excessive busyness. I didn't seem to notice that every part of my body was screaming, "I'm exhausted!"

I ignored my body's cry for rest. Then, I was thrown out on the hard road of reality when my body completely shut down during a speaking engagement to a group of teenage girls. There I was, speaking about spiritual excellence as I fell over on the floor! (No, I was not slain in the Spirit!) I was taken to the doctor and diagnosed with Epstein-Barr virus, more commonly known as chronic fatigue syndrome. My immune system had completely shut down; I was so exhausted that I could hardly lift my head off the pillow. The doctor informed me that I would have to stop all activity—in other words, pull my lifestyle out of fifth gear and put it in park.

There I stood face to face with the fear that I'd really blown it this time, that I might never regain my health and energy again. After everything that God had done for me, I felt guilty going to Him and asking Him to fix what I had broken again.

Every day as I lay there, I'd cry. I didn't get to play with my little boy, go to church, or go out with my friends. I missed ministering. And although many people prayed for me, my Epstein-Barr virus felt worse. Prior to contracting this virus, I had been able to push through any and all obstacles that got in the way of my goals. The word *health* took on a much more significant meaning for me. This was one thing that was completely out of my control.

After weeks of lying in bed depressed and sick, I begged God to show me if there was any way to heal my body. I did a little research on sickness and disease and found that the main killers of our day—heart disease, cancer, and diabetes—were practically nonexistent three generations ago when tuberculosis, pneumonia, and dysentery were the big threat to health. Recently new ailments have joined the battle to steal our health, like obesity, chronic fatigue, arthritis, and digestive problems. I came to the conclusion that in spite of all the scientific advances and extra wisdom we're supposed to have in our current times, we must still be missing something!

I began to research and compare differences between biblical diets and the mainstream modern America diet of today. I found that the biblical diet consisted mainly of raw fruits, raw vegetables, raw seeds, whole grains, and occasional meats and fish. (See Genesis 1:29.) Throughout recorded history, the menu remained basically the same.

Interestingly, today we see that every study done in the last thirty years on diet, health, and disease prevention points without fail to the same time-tested diet written thousands of years ago by—who else?—the God who created our bodies.

Prompted by the Holy Spirit, I went to my kitchen and pulled out all of the sugar-free, fat-free foods that I was eating and read each ingredient listed on the labels. How much of my daily intake was fresh food and how much was pre-packaged, microwaveable munchies? I followed this with research on the Internet, looking for exactly what was in my food and how it was affecting my body.

I was shocked to find that most of the things I was eating weren't really food at all and had little or no nutritional value. Basically, they were processed poisons, preservatives, drugs, and chemicals cleverly disguised as edibles by ingenious marketeers.

If you're suffering from severe exhaustion or have been diagnosed with chronic fatigue syndrome as I have, the following information may be of great value to you. The information is not based on my opinion but on scientific studies, *but it also is not intended to replace the advise of a qualified health professional!*

THE GREAT AMERICAN RAT EXPERIMENT

The following is an account of an interesting three-part experiment comparing the effects of raw food versus cooked food on rats. This account is taken from a book titled *Goldot* by Lewis E. Cook, Jr. and Junko Yasui:

> It has been found that a group of rats that were fed diets of raw vegetables, fruits and nuts, and whole grains from birth grew into completely healthy specimens and never suffered from any disease. They were never ill. They grew rapidly, but never became fat, mated with enthusiasm and had healthy offspring. They were always gently affectionate and playful and lived in perfect harmony with each other. Upon reaching an old age, equivalent to eighty years in humans, these rats were put to death and autopsied. At that advanced age their organs, glands, tissues, and all body processes appeared to be in perfect condition without any sign of aging or deterioration.
>
> A companion group of rats were fed a diet comparable to that of the average American and included white bread, cooked foods, meats, milk, salt, soft drinks, candies, cakes, vitamins and other supplements, medicines for their ailments, etc. During their lifetime these rats became fat and, from the earliest age, contracted most of the diseases of modern American society including colds, fever, pneumonia, poor vision, cataracts, heart disease, arthritis, cancer, and many more.
>
> Most of this group died prematurely at early ages but during their lifetime most of them were vicious, snarling beasts, fighting with one another, stealing one another's food and attempting to kill each other. They had to be kept apart to prevent total destruction of the entire group. Their offspring were all sick and exhibited the same general characteristics as the parents.

As this group of rats died one by one or in epidemics of various diseases, autopsies were performed revealing extensive degenerative conditions in every part of their bodies. All organs, glands, and tissues were affected as were the skin, hair, blood, and nervous system. They were all truly total physical and nervous wrecks. The same conditions existed in the few that survived the full duration of the experiment.[1]

ABOUT SUGAR . . .

After reading that, I did further research on sugar, chemical sweeteners, and flour. Because of my love for desserts, the first subject I tackled was sugar. I was angry and disappointed to find out that sugar is a drug and extremely harmful to the body. When it's consumed, it ferments in the body, causing the formation of carbonic acid, which is destructive to the cells, causing nerve damage and deteriorating brain function. It also contributes to breaking down the immune system, causing depression, headaches, moodiness, exhaustion, chronic fatigue, premature aging, burning out the adrenal glands, loss of concentration, hypoglycemia, and, at worst, diabetes. As if that weren't enough, I learned that this fat-free drug called "sugar" turns into fat.

The average person consumes one hundred thirty pounds of refined sugar each year. When we stop eating this poison, our body actually detoxes, much the same way alcoholics or drug addicts detox when they stop drinking or using drugs. Sugar is disguised in many forms. Brown sugar is simply refined sugar sprayed with molasses to appear more whole.

Turbinado sugar, which gives the illusion of health, is just one step away from white sugar. It's 95 percent sucrose. Another disguise is high fructose corn syrup. This is a cheap and plentiful sweetener often used in soft drinks, candy, and baked goods.

Corn syrup is found almost everywhere, including spaghetti

sauce, ketchup, and even some juices labeled "natural." Corn syrup, processed from corn starch, is almost as sweet as refined sugar. It's absorbed quickly by the blood. It also contains high levels of pesticide residue and common allergens.

ABOUT ASPARTAME . . .

I was addicted to diet sodas, so the next thing I looked up was *aspartame*. It's found in artificial sweeteners and most foods labeled "sugar-free." Aspartame is based on two amino acids that might seem natural; however, according to scientists, a quick dose of two isolated amino acids could harm you, especially if you are dehydrated.

According to the FDA, aspartame accounts for over 85 percent of all adverse reactions to food additives reported to the U.S. Food and Drug Administration. The list of seventy-three side effects attributed to aspartame include seizures, dizziness, migraine headaches, nausea, numbness, weight gain, depression, fatigue, breathing difficulties, joint pain, hemorrhaging of the eyes, anxiety attacks, behavioral changes in children, and even death! Studies have shown that users of aspartame gain weight rather than lose it, and other evidence suggests that it actually increases the appetite.

ABOUT WHITE FLOUR . . .

Believe it or not, white flour is bleached with the same ingredients that we use to bleach our clothes and purify our swimming pools. Manufacturers take whole grains, remove the bran, remove the wheat germ, and then bleach the remaining flour white. This means that our breads and pastas are made from a substance lacking nutritional value and fiber and are processed with bleach. What's interesting is that the manufacturers take the good stuff—the bran and wheat germ—and sell it back to us as "health food." White flour is in most bagels, breads, and almost all pastas.

ABOUT NITRATES AND HORMONES IN MEATS . . .

I looked up the word *nitrate*. Nitrates are used to preserve and enhance meats such as packaged turkey, bacon, hot dogs, and bologna, but they have the opposite effect on people who eat them. Nitrates turn into nitrosamines in the body and have been connected to childhood leukemia, brain tumors, and stomach cancer.

While studying about nitrates in meats, I discovered that many meats also have artificial growth hormones in them. The use of growth hormones can produce larger and leaner animals more rapidly than nature ever intended, but the effects can be very dangerous to our health.

ABOUT CAFFEINE . . .

I learned that caffeine depletes the body's B vitamins, which are essential to maintaining your body's immune system. Caffeine contributes to bladder and stomach cancer, raises blood pressure, increases heart rate, aggravates diabetes, and increases PMS symptoms. Caffeine is found in coffee, tea, some soft drinks, and chocolate. People with chronic fatigue syndrome should avoid caffeine at all costs.

SO WHAT'S LEFT?

After my discoveries I became discouraged because I love all of the above so-called foods. I began to battle in my mind, *Am I willing to give these things up so I can win my health back?* It was definitely a war between my flesh and my spirit. My flesh did not want to die, but if I didn't give up the food, it would have died anyway.

As stupid as this sounds, I actually began to pray to God, not for strength, but for wisdom on what I should do and what I should eat. *I was happier in my ignorance before I knew the facts!* I was hoping that a miracle pill and some rest would restore my health. Again I was faced with a choice. Was I going to continue to feed my flesh poisonous foods that tasted great, or was I going to sacrifice the food that held my taste buds captive so I could be fit for my King? As I lay there struggling, I realized that God had sacrificed His only Son so I could have eternal life. The least I could do was sacrifice the tasty "trash food" I loved.

TIME FOR A CHANGE

I knew it was time to change my eating habits. I decided to put the Genesis 1:29 diet to the test. I took all the food that was labeled sugar-free and fat-free out of my house. The King had prepared a table for His children, and I was going to eat from it. I cut out all white flour, white sugar, processed food, artificial sweeteners, caffeine, dairy products, and tap water. To give up these foods was the hardest battle I'd ever fought against my flesh, because no matter where you go, it's hard to escape these foods. However, it was a battle worth winning. In eight weeks of cutting out these "fake" foods, I was able to lose the twenty-three pounds I gained lying in bed, I conquered my chronic fatigue, and I entered the Mrs. USA pageant to win the crown. The benefits were unbelievable. My skin looked so healthy that I didn't have to wear foundation. My hair thickened. My energy level was incredible. Today, I am thankful that my body taught me how to listen. If you're experiencing exhaustion, sickness, or have been diagnosed with chronic fatigue syndrome, I pray you will utilize and benefit from the "Eating for Energy" plan found on pages 93–97.

BODY TALK . . . LISTEN!

If you're like me, you've probably tried everything possible to find enough energy to make it through the day. Coffee, sugar, pep pills . . . there's plenty of artificial and natural stimulants to choose from, but the problem is that our adrenal glands will soon burn out and our entire immune system ends up broken down. When this happens, sickness and disease eventually win in our battle for health and energy.

Don't look to a substance to keep you healthy; listen to your body! God put a silent voice inside of us that starts with a whisper and gets louder the longer we ignore it. It starts with physical discomfort like headaches, indigestion, and a need for rest. If we do not listen, our body talks louder by communicating through sicknesses and severe exhaustion. If we continue to ignore it, it screams, "Breakdown! I can't take anymore!" Is your body talking to you? Ask yourself the following questions.

1. Does your body wake up refreshed?
2. Does your body have energy throughout the day?
3. How does your body feel after you eat a meal?
4. How does your body feel mid-afternoon?
5. At the end of your work day, does your body have enough energy to enjoy your evening?
6. Do you sleep well?
7. Does your body feel achy?
8. Do you get headaches often?
9. Do you go from one flu to the next?
10. Do you have digestive problems?
11. Do you have allergies such as runny nose or puffy eyes?

WARNING SIGNS

When you experience any of these things, your body is talking to you. It's telling you, "Something is not right. Please help me!" These symptoms are not normal. It's your body trying to get rid of the toxins you have been putting inside of it. THESE ARE WARNING SIGNS! The tragedy is that most of us don't take the warning signs seriously. We justify them by making excuses until one day it's too late to turn back. If you're sick and tired of being sick and tired, you're going to have to do more than complain about it or try to drug yourself back to health. You must begin eating for excellence.

God desires us to be in good health. Third John 2 says, "Beloved, I wish above all things that thou mayest prosper and be in health, even as thy soul prospereth" (KJV). The road is wide that leads to destruction. The path to the crown of health is narrow. Don't look to man's shortcuts—look to God's long-term plan for a long, healthy life! He loves you and longs to bless you, but He can't reward disobedience when you make His temple your trash can.

Our society has been programmed into thinking that we can put anything we want into our bodies, abuse our bodies, neglect our bodies, and then when our bodies break down, all we have to do is run to the doctor who will give us a magic pill. In just a few days, we will be all better.

The truth is, it just doesn't work that way. We need to take responsibility and do our part to take care of God's temple or we will never experience the blessing of good health.

EATING FOR ENERGY

The following is the daily routine I used to help me conquer chronic fatigue syndrome:

Morning:

First thing in the morning, I drink one glass of water with one tablespoon of green barley powder* mixed in it. Immediately following the green barley, I drink another large glass of water.

Breakfast:

Example 1: Scrambled hormone-free, fertile eggs with onions, tomatoes, and red bell peppers. A slice of sprouted

---

*Green barley powder is a "cell food" that contains the widest spectrum of vitamins, minerals, and enzymes of any food on earth. The green barley I use was invented by Dr. Yoshihide Hagiwara, M.D., the Japanese research pharmacologist. I have found this to be of great benefit to me to handle my busy lifestyle.

yeast-free bread and a cup of herbal iced tea.

Example 2: A small bowl of oatmeal sweetened with honey and topped with raw slivered almonds; one scrambled hormone-free, fertile egg.

Example 3: A blended shake made with protein powder, rice milk, a little decaffeinated coffee, a chocolate-flavored healthy shake mix, and crushed ice. It tastes similar to a frozen cappuccino drink.

After I get my little boy off to school and my husband to work, I take time to feed on the Word (the Bible) and pray.

Noon:

For lunch, I always eat raw food so I have the energy to make it through the rest of my day.

Example: Green salad with lots of different vegetables, salad dressing on the side (I never use the diet dressings because they taste terrible and they're full of sugars, salts, and chemicals), and a flavored rice cake or a few rye crackers. Sometimes I include chicken or raw nuts for protein. Herbal iced tea or mineral water to drink.

Afternoon:

The afternoon is my weakest time of the day. I always crave something sweet, so I usually eat a small cup of nondairy frozen yogurt or some sliced-up fruit; I drink a glass of mineral water over ice, with sliced lemon. I also make another glass of green barley powder mixed with water for energy.

Evening:

I usually try to set a pretty table for my family with candles, place mats, and the whole works. This atmosphere helps me to relax and enjoy dinner with my family. We love to barbecue, and we try to do it at least a couple times per week. My dinner normally includes a small portion of protein (tofu or lean hormone-free beef or chicken), small raw salad, sweet potato, baked potato or brown rice, and a healthy dessert (sweetened with honey, molasses, pure maple syrup, or sliced fruit).

Bedtime:

I try not to eat or drink anything before I fall asleep so I don't wake up bloated. If I do eat anything, it's just a nibble of protein or yeast-free bread.

EATING FOR ENERGY SUCCESS TIPS

- *Water:* We can live up to forty days without food, but we cannot live more than four days without water. Water helps cleanse the body of toxins. It brings oxygen to the blood. It helps create beautiful skin, hydrates our bodies, and is necessary for fat loss. To this day, the only things I drink are water, mineral water, and herbal teas.
- *Exercise:* I try to exercise for at least twenty to thirty minutes each day because of the body's need for oxygen. Exercising thirty minutes a day is one of the greatest gifts we can give to our body. It helps improve our health, brings life-giving oxygen to our cells, increases our energy, cleans our lymph glands, evens out our blood sugars, enhances our ability to manage stress and depression, improves our strength and endurance, adds healthy years to our lives, burns fat calories, and rids our body of harmful toxins. Without daily vigorous exercise:

1. *Tissue cells lose their elasticity.*
2. *Lymph cannot move adequately to cleanse and feed body cells.*

3. *Muscles decrease in size and waste away.*
4. *The body does not receive a sufficient supply of oxygen.*

God breathed into Adam the breath of life and the dead heap of minerals sprang to life. Oxygen is absolutely necessary to produce life in Adam. It is that same oxygen that is absolutely vital and necessary to sustain life in man today.

—DR. GEORGE H. MALKMUS

- Any recipe can be made into a healthy recipe by replacing white sugar with honey or molasses.
- Replace white flour with barley or whole-wheat flour (if you're not allergic to wheat).
- Use monounsaturated oil (pure virgin olive oil, cold-pressed canola, or unprocessed vegetable oil). Don't use saturated oils.
- Replace dairy with nondairy rice beverages and nondairy cheeses made with tofu.
- Replace sugary cereals with whole-grain cereals, oatmeal, Cream of Wheat, and Cream of Rice.
- Eat less animal protein and eat more raw nuts, soy, tofu, and tempura.
- Replace salt with onion powder, garlic powder, and Bragg's liquid amino acids.
- Eat raw food as much as possible, avoiding packaged and processed foods. Read the labels and remember: Live food makes you feel alive!
- Drink at least eight to ten glasses of water a day—distilled or purified only.
- Take the junk food out of your house.
- If you cannot find or afford organic fruits and vegetables, soak them in a pure form of citrus extract found in most health food stores.

WARNING: If you decide to remove any of the following

ingredients from your diet (bleached flour, refined sugar, or caffeine), your body will begin to detox. Don't be alarmed if you experience light headaches and achiness and maybe even feel worse for a few days. During detox, increase your distilled water intake to ten to twelve glasses a day and try to get more rest during this time. Once the detox symptoms have passed, your head will clear and you'll feel an energy like you've never known. I have found that when I stick to this routine, the benefits have been well worth the sacrifice. I realize that it is difficult to stick to a program this strict every day. Do the very best you can to eat as healthy as possible.

•••••••••••••••••••••••••••••
Rest Stop

1. What is your body trying to say to you? List your symptoms.

2. Ask God to show you if you need to censor out any foods or make any changes in your lifestyle.

3. Write out what you feel God is showing you.

4. Write a prayer to God for strength and find someone to hold you accountable. Remember, just as with food addictions and eating disorders, this too will be a fight you will not be able to win alone.

1. Lewis E. Cook, Jr. and Junko Yasui, *Goldot,* n.p., n.d.

8

Don't Forget Your Gifts!

I used to think I didn't have any gifts or talents. Almost everything I tried, I failed in. When I was eighteen, I tried waitressing, but on my first day on the job I dropped a spinach salad on a man's head. I was fired on the spot. After that, I tried attending beauty college, but I almost drowned a woman at the shampoo bowl when I shot water from the water hose up her nose. I took dance lessons, and the instructor told me I was too uncoordinated and asked me to leave the class. I wasn't good in school because I suffer from dyslexia—I see things backwards. I try to be organized, but by the end of the week, my home looks like a tornado hit it. Even when I go on an organizational binge, in a short time I can't remember where I put anything.

It never occurred to me that my passion to communicate with people and to encourage others was the God-given gift that motivates my spirit. The only thing I love to do more than eat is talk. Generally speaking, I'm generally speaking. I have one gift—it's my big mouth—and I praise

God that I get to use my gift frequently!

I love gifts. I love giving gifts. I love receiving gifts. The greatest gift I've ever received is the gift God gave me through His Son, Jesus Christ. It is my salvation. It is your salvation. All we have to do is receive it! But God has given you another gift. Your "gift" is a divine mixture of God-given strengths and special abilities that motivate your spirit to respond to life in a certain way. Your gift enables you to experience more success in life and build up others in the body of Christ.

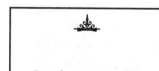

In order to accomplish His goals, God created us totally unique and equipped our spirit with certain personality characteristics.

Unfortunately, our physical abilities and talents often get the most attention because our minds are naturally "tuned" to things that are seen. So, likewise, we don't recognize our God-given spiritual gift as a special ability; our minds are not naturally "tuned" to the things of the Spirit.

As we do recognize our gift, we begin to experience great freedom. We begin to understand why we perceive things the way we do! From this freedom, we develop a passion to use our gift to be a blessing—a present—to others. We're inspired and empowered to move far beyond anything we could dream in the physical realm.

In Paul's letter to the Christians in Rome, we see that not only are our bodies living sacrifices to be presented to God, but we each have a unique place to work within His body because of our spirit's gift.

> Therefore, I urge you, brothers, in view of God's mercy, to offer your bodies as living sacrifices, holy and pleasing to God—this is your spiritual act of worship. Do not conform any longer to the pattern of this world, but be transformed by the renewing of your mind. Then you will be able to test and approve what

God's will is—his good, pleasing and perfect will.

For by the grace given me I say to every one of you: Do not think of yourself more highly than you ought, but rather think of yourself with sober judgment, in accordance with the measure of faith God has given you. Just as each of us has one body with many members, and these members do not all have the same function, so in Christ we who are many form one body, and each member belongs to all the others. We have different gifts, according to the grace given us. If a man's gift is prophesying, let him use it in proportion to his faith. If it is serving, let him serve; if it is teaching, let him teach; if it is encouraging [exhorting], let him encourage; if it is contributing [giving] to the needs of others, let him give generously; if it is leadership [administration], let him govern diligently; if it is showing mercy, let him do it cheerfully.

—ROMANS 12:1–8

There are seven motivational gifts. These are "spiritual endowments" that we possess, each one being different because they each have unique and specific functions within the body.

This "spiritual endowment" we have each received is given because of God's grace and has nothing to do with whether we deserve it or not. It is given to us by God out of His love for us. This undeserved grace is important to remember, because our natural tendency is to boast about how "gifted" we are. It is for this reason that Paul warns us not to think "too highly" of ourselves.

If we look closely, we see that each of these seven motivational gifts also falls into one of two categories:

1. *Speaking gifts:* prophecy (perceiving and proclaiming truth); teaching (researching, protecting, and explaining truth); and exhorting (encouraging, motivating).

2. *Serving gifts:* administration (organizing, leading, directing—can often function in the speaking category as well); serving (doing, working); giving (contributing, benefiting, imparting); mercy (compassion, feeling).

Along with motivational gifts, there are also ministerial gifts and manifestation gifts.

> There are different kinds of gifts [spiritual endowments], but the same Spirit. There are different kinds of service [ministries, function, or offices], but the same Lord. There are different kinds of working [manifestations, effects, or results], but the same God works all of them in all men.
> —1 CORINTHIANS 12:4–6

MINISTRY GIFTS

Ministry gifts are an office we hold or a place where we function or serve. You may have a pastor who has the motivational gift of exhortation or prophecy but also serves in the office of teacher. Or you may have the motivational gift of compassion, but you are currently serving or functioning in a ministerial role or office as a server (nurse, laborer, secretary).

Ephesians 4:11 says that Jesus gave ministry or office gifts (apostles, prophets, evangelists, pastors, and teachers) to build up and equip the body of Christ.

MANIFESTATION GIFTS

Each of us can function in a variety of areas and produce different effects or results. These are called manifestation gifts. The emphasis as we see from 1 Corinthians is not on us, but on the person benefiting from the gift and on God who is doing the work (manifestation or effect) to meet a specific need. We also notice that God can meet these needs through whomever He chooses. These effects are listed in the following verses:

> Now to each one the manifestation of the Spirit is given for the common good. To one there is given through the Spirit the message of wisdom, to another the message of knowledge by means of the same Spirit, to another faith by the same Spirit, to another gifts of healing by that one Spirit, to another miraculous powers, to another prophecy, to another distinguishing between spirits, to another speaking in different kinds of tongues, and to still another the interpretation of tongues. All these are the work of one and the same Spirit, and he gives to each one just as he determines.
> —1 CORINTHIANS 12:7–11

There can be much more said about ministerial office gifts and manifestation gifts, but we're going to examine and understand our motivational gifts. It is there that we see our specific passion, purpose, and place in this world and in the body of Christ.

Part of the miracle of God's creation is that we're created in God's image. We have a choice to live our lives accepting and using our motivational gift in service to Him, neglecting or even abusing our gift by pursuing our own interests, or by working in an area in which we are *not* gifted. When we are operating within our gift, it doesn't feel like work; it feels natural because it's what we were created to do. It's how we're wired. God saw each of us before we were born because He is the one who formed and created us. (See Psalm 139:16–17.)

He knows all about us. He also knows that *who we are*—the person we become—can be influenced by many factors. The three most influential factors are:

1. *The gifting that our spirit has received from Him.*

102

2. *Our family's attitudes and actions and our rela-tionships with them.* (That includes our parents, grandparents, brothers, and sisters.)
3. *The influences of the world and the culture around us.*

It's possible that we don't even realize how much these factors have affected us. Many of us have never stopped to consider who we really are or the areas in which we are gifted. We stumble through life unfulfilled, taking roads that lead us away from God's plan for us. How, then, do we know what our gift is? I'm pretty sure that when I was born the doctor didn't hold me up by the ankles, slap me on the behind, and exclaim, "Congratulations! You have an eight-and-one-half-pound baby exhorter!"

We can learn what our gifts are by observing our be-havior, thoughts, and attitudes toward life. As you read through this book, my hope is that the Lord will teach you about yourself and the special abilities and motivational gift with which He has blessed you. Knowing and understanding our spirit's motivational gift and the motivational gifts of others will help us in these four areas:

1. *It helps us to understand our "spirit" and how God can and will use us.*

For we are God's workmanship, created in Christ Jesus to do good works, which God prepared in advance for us to do.

—EPHESIANS 2:10

My husband and I have always felt, from day one, that God wanted us to minister together. The first eight years of our marriage, however, we struggled and fought because we were so different. If it hadn't been for an increased understanding of our spiritual gifts and our difference by design, we would have probably killed each other by now!

103

2. *It helps us receive what God wants to show us through others.*

My stepmom Susie helped me lose weight and get in shape when I was a teenager. Her gift of administration made her bold and strong enough to help me stick to my goals. I can see how God used her at that difficult time in my life.

3. *It prevents us from making unhealthy comparisons with others.*

We are all guilty of this. We observe someone who is exceptionally talented in one area, and we beat ourselves up because we're not as good. Or, we'll somehow point out their weaknesses to make us feel better.

I used to agonize that I wasn't more organized. I had a friend who just hated talking on the phone to people. We can sit around and berate each other (or ourselves) for our weaknesses, or we understand them and walk in the freedom that God has gifted each of our spirits differently. Ideally, we can draw on each other's special skills and increase our effectiveness in building up the body of Christ.

4. *It makes it easier to see the areas we personally need to change to be more like Christ.*

My best friend Joyce can sit and listen for hours when counseling someone. God has blessed her with the gift of compassion and mercy; if there's an altar call, Joyce will be there and stay for hours listening, feeling, and hurting with people.

I, on the other hand, have the gift of talking. I'd rather expend all my energy giving a powerful, encouraging message, and then talk some more, until I'm ready to collapse!

....

Rest Stop

1. Before you read the next chapter, spend a moment reflecting on the talents and abilities that make you "you." Would other people in your life agree?

9

What's Inside Your Present?

Okay, so maybe you passed the last "rest stop" because you're not sure what your giftings are. Maybe you haven't yet realized that *you are a gift*—a present—created by God and given as a gift to touch the lives of those around you. In the following verses, Paul speaks of seven gifts known as the *motivational gifts:*

> We have different gifts, according to the grace given us. If a man's gift is prophesying, let him use it in proportion to his faith. If it is serving, let him serve; if it is teaching, let him teach; if it is encouraging [exhorting], let him encourage; if it is contributing to the needs of others, let him give generously; if it is leadership [administration], let him govern diligently; if it is showing mercy, let him do it cheerfully.
>
> —ROMANS 12:6–8

THE PROPHET

Prophet: (prah -fit) n. one who perceives, proclaims or one who foretells.

- If you tend to be direct and frank, if you feel compelled to tell people what you really think, you might have the gift of prophecy.
- If you are confident that your point of view is the right point of view, you might have the gift of prophecy.
- If you stay true to your convictions no matter who disagrees with you, you might have the gift of prophecy.
- If you wait impatiently for others to "get their act together," you might have the gift of prophecy.
- If you tend to see things as black or white and are reluctant to see "gray" areas, you might have the gift of prophecy.

Every morning, just before dawn, on farms from every corner of the world, a strange and compulsive urge overtakes the male chicken—commonly called a rooster. He is uniquely inspired to announce the coming of the sun and is strongly motivated to do so—in spite of the wishes of any other barnyard creatures. In much the same way, a prophet must proclaim his personal convictions.

A prophet's words, as we see in Jeremiah, are like fire and can be used to tear down and uproot or to build and plant. When a prophet is truly led by the Spirit of God, there is nothing more inspiring. Whether the result—or effect—is healing, repentance, deliverance, or judgment, it will always be astounding because it is led by the Holy Spirit.

A Prophet's Strengths . . .

- Able to discern true commitment

- Aggressive speech (need to be, to stand up and speak for God)
- Able to grasp concepts
- Willing to be condemned for doing right
- Strong desire to inform others
- Responsive to spiritual conviction

A Prophet's Weaknesses . . .

- Quick to judge (strong tendency to be critical)
- Needs to be alert and sensitive to the reactions of others
- Needs to verify his positions with Scripture
- Focuses on negatives
- Pride in personal abilities
- Needs to develop meekness
- Intolerant of other's pain (lack of sympathy)

Things a Prophet Might Say . . .

If you were to follow a prophet around and eavesdrop on some conversations, you might hear comments similar to the following:

- "Don't you get it?"
- "I'm not being judgmental—I'm just speaking the truth!"
- "Just get over it, would you!"
- "I just have to tell you what God wants for you!"
- "You don't have to understand it—just do it!"
- "I really don't care what they say—it's the right thing to do!"

Prophet Last Seen . . .

If you're on the lookout, here's where you might commonly find someone with the gift of prophecy:

- Arguing a case in court
- Behind a pulpit
- In the cockpit
- *Fortune 500* magazine
- In a police officer's uniform
- In politics
- In the military, commanding
- Behind TV news microphone
- On the mission field
- Teaching rules or regulations
- CEO of his own company

....
Rest Stop

1. By observing the behavior and attitudes of the people in your life, who would you say might have the gift of prophecy? What three characteristics come to mind first that might reveal this to you? List them below.

2. Notice the weaknesses of the prophet. Have you been hurt (your spirit bruised) by a prophet's insensitive comments or aggressive speech? Please note some examples and try to identify some of the emotions you felt.

3. Can knowing their gift help you to build or strengthen a spirit-to-spirit relationship with them? How?

4. Can you see why knowing YOUR gift will help you to see how and why they relate to you in the way they do?

5. What could God be trying to teach you through their gifting?

THE SERVER

Server: (ser ver) n. one who serves; gifted in the area of service.

- If you're a tireless worker and don't even mind working alone, you might have the gift of serving.
- If you overlook your own personal needs because you're too busy helping others, you might have the gift of serving.
- If you'd rather vacuum the church than speak in church, you might have the gift of serving.
- If it bothers you when others don't see or seem to care about an obvious need, you might have the gift of serving.
- If you have a hard time saying *no* to committees, service groups, or the requests of others, you might have the gift of serving.

If you've ever put a drop of oil on a puddle of clean water, you'll notice that it will scurry around like crazy as if it is trying to cover as much surface area as possible. You can't contain it or stop it without a desperate plan. That's the kind of energy a server seems to have when it comes to work. They are strongly motivated to cover as much area as they can until they are completely expended. If you have a project that needs to get done involving manual labor (typing, cleaning, moving, filing, painting), you absolutely must find a server! I've never seen a harder worker than my dear friend and business manager, Lana. She works around the clock and regularly skips meals to finish projects—usually mine!

A Server's Strengths . . .

- Tireless worker
- Extremely loyal
- Excellent at perceiving and anticipating needs
- A good memory for details pertinent to other's needs
- Loves helping others
- Conscious of thriftiness
- A willingness to use personal funds to prevent hindering a project

A Server's Weaknesses . . .

- Tends to disapprove of other's inabilities
- Overlooks personal problem areas (including family) because they're too busy helping
- Needs to develop leadership qualities (rather *do* than *delegate*)
- Never-ending "To-do" list
- Can't say *no,* even to needs that are not his or hers to meet
- Tends to have lower-digestive tract problems because of stress
- Feels rejection when services aren't needed
- Needs to be willing to let others serve him or her
- Has low self-esteem (need to work to gain approval)
- Has trouble cutting children's apron strings

Things a Server Might Say . . .

If you were to follow a server around and eavesdrop on some conversations, you might hear comments similar to the following:

- "Let me do that for you."

- "It's no trouble at all; I planned on being up late anyway."
- "I thought you might need this . . . "
- "I'll get something to eat later. I've got these things on my list to get done first."
- "No, thanks, I'd feel much better if I just did it myself."

Server Last Seen . . .

If you're on the lookout, here's where you might commonly find someone with the gift of serving:

- Any volunteer committee
- Service organizations
- Vocational trade or manual labor jobs
- Hand-crafting their Christmas gifts
- Fixing their neighbor's car, roof, or furnace
- Mowing, cooking, or vacuuming for someone else
- Doing laundry or sewing for their adult son or daughter

Rest Stop

1. By observing the behavior and attitudes of the people in your life, who would you say might have the gift of serving? What three characteristics come to mind first that might reveal this to you? List them below.

2. Notice the weaknesses of the server. Have you experienced any conflict with a server because of these weaknesses? Please note some examples and try to identify some of the emotions you felt.

3. Can knowing their gift help you to build or strengthen a spirit-to-spirit relationship with them? How?

4. Can you see why knowing YOUR gift will help you to see how and why they relate to you in the way they do?

5. What could God be trying to teach you through their gifting?

THE TEACHER

Teacher: (tee -tchr) n. one who researches, explains, and imparts wisdom.

- If research is more exciting to you than building relationships, you might have the gift of teaching.
- If you're compelled to discover knowledge and make vital information available to others, you might have the gift of teaching.
- If you're known as the neighborhood expert on something, you might have the gift of teaching.
- If you're self-controlled and not easily ruffled, you might have the gift of teaching.
- If it bugs you when people stretch the truth or use Scripture out of context, you might have the gift of teaching.

One of the things that attracted me to my husband, Steve, was his temperament. He was calm and rational, very smart, and easy to understand. He was the perfect balance to my crazy personality.

At first, we worked great together. I was often in a position to speak publicly, and because I barely made it through school, I asked Steve to help me on my grammar, my speech, and my writing. I now know better. Steve's natural ability to see what was wrong with something (usually me) and his weakness at being sensitive and relational turned out to be a huge struggle for us. What he thought was helping was actually hurting. Now we're learning to be sensitive to and appreciative of each other's strengths and weaknesses so that we can better minister to each other.

A Teacher's Strengths . . .

- The watchdog of the Christian community
- Delights in detailed studies (asks the tough questions)
- Knows his stuff (not opinions)
- Serious nature (dry sense of humor)
- Looks beyond the words to the context
- Not easily swayed (needs lots of facts and time to make decisions)
- Quick mind for deductions
- Mellow temperament
- Cool, steady, great to be around during pressure, not easily ruffled
- Great conversationalist for those who are searching
- Key words are, "For those who are searching!"
- Self-disciplined

A Teacher's Weaknesses . . .

- Consumed by facts and gaining knowledge but lacks personal application
- Thinks that others will function better if informed by their teaching
- More interested in research than people
- More interested in libraries than parties

- Feels above restrictions, "I think a two-year in-depth study on the devil will be helpful . . . "

Things a Teacher Might Say . . .

If you were to follow a teacher around and eavesdrop on some conversations, you might hear comments similar to the following:

- "Let me show you an easier way to do that."
- "Actually, it would be much more accurate if . . . "
- "You go ahead and shop, honey; I'll be in the bookstore."
- "Johnny, I'm only going to explain this one more time."
- "Let's be logical about this, OK?"

Teacher Last Seen . . .

If you're on the lookout, here's where you might commonly find someone with the gift of teaching:

- Buried in books at the library or browsing at the bookstore
- Surfing on the Internet
- In a research lab
- Behind a typewriter
- In front of a congregation or a class of students

••••••••••••••••••••••••••
Rest Stop

1. By observing the behavior and attitudes of the people in your life, who would you say might have the gift of teaching? What three characteristics come to mind first that might reveal this to you? List them below.

2. Notice the weaknesses of the teacher. Have you been hurt (your spirit bruised) because of a teacher with these weaknesses? (Perhaps they made critical or judgmental comments about you.) Please note some examples and try to identify some of the emotions you felt.

3. Can knowing their gift help you to build or strengthen a spirit-to-spirit relationship with them? How?

4. Can you see why knowing YOUR gift will help you to see how and why they relate to you in the way they do?

5. What could God be trying to teach you through their gifting?

THE EXHORTER

Exhorter: (eg -zôrt´ ẽr) one who urges earnestly; entreats and encourages.

- If you make friends easily and can find common ground with anybody, but you avoid conflicts at all costs, you might have the gift of exhortation.
- If you love to make someone's day by encouraging them or praising them, you might have the gift of exhortation.
- If you dive into relationships and can't say *no* for fear of not being accepted, you might have the gift of exhortation.

- If you're an excellent communicator and gifted salesperson but tend to bend the truth a little to make things sound more interesting, you might have the gift of exhortation.
- If you're spontaneous and fun and think rules were made for other people, you might have the gift of exhortation.

Whenever I go to a sporting event like a basketball game or a football game, I get a kick out of watching the cheerleaders—especially high school cheerleaders. They are endless bundles of energy who jump and dance and flap their arms in a spirited attempt to get the crowd pumped up and feeling good about the team. Many times these young "go-getters" are clueless about what the athletes are doing behind them, but that doesn't slow them down one bit. "Go, team! Fight! Get that ball!" Their bright, cheery faces and constant movement always add life to their sometimes choreographed, sometimes improvised performances. These are the girls who never run short on friends at school and thrive when there's an audience. Proudly encouraging. Loudly motivating. Never boring. Always "up" for the big game. These girls are the designated exhorters. When I think back to when I was in school, I always wanted to be a cheerleader, but I was just too unpopular and overweight. Besides, I hate to admit it . . . but, back then, my druggie friends and I had our own ideas about getting "up" for a game.

An Exhorter's Strengths . . .

- Anxious to please
- Avoids conflicts at all costs
- Has trouble saying *no*
- Sees importance of individuals
- Great networkers
- Easily finds common ground with others
- Dives into relationships

- Positive outlook (can joke or laugh about situations)
- Extremely dedicated when focused and interested in something
- Spontaneous and creative
- Quick to grab solutions
- Very convincing (even if they make it up)
- Quick to give advice
- Good at word pictures
- Wants to write a book
- Encouraging speaker and strong motivator
- Communicates effectively
- Makes friends easily (very charismatic)
- Concerned about personal application of biblical principles

An Exhorter's Weaknesses . . .

- Bends convictions to gain approval (in spite of facts)
- Makes promises not able to keep
- Doesn't take life seriously (lots of ups and downs)
- Can become defensive and retaliatory to get focus off herself
- Easy to live in denial
- Closed spirit in confrontations
- Difficult taking criticism
- Beats herself up
- Reserved in commitments to people
- Spontaneity may disrupt other's lives
- Difficulty following and respecting rules and important details
- Difficulty sitting still to read, study, or listen to presentations

Things an Exhorter Might Say . . .

If you were to follow an exhorter around and eavesdrop

on some conversations, you might hear comments similar to the following:

- "Let's do it anyway; it will be fun!"
- "Outline? What outline? Who needs an outline?"
- "I finally found my keys . . . now, where did I put my car?"
- "Sure it can be done . . . just leave it to me!"
- "How can you expect me to clean the house when a friend needed me?"

Exhorter Last Seen . . .

If you're on the lookout, here's where you might commonly find someone with the gift of exhortation:

- Car dealerships or other sales position
- On any platform
- TV talk show host
- Hyping another brilliant idea
- On the phone
- Running late
- Asking for directions
- Karaoke clubs and talent shows

Rest Stop

1. By observing the behavior and attitudes of the people in your life, who would you say might have the gift of exhortation? What three characteristics come to mind first that might reveal this to you? List them below.

2. Notice the weaknesses of the exhorter. Have you experienced any conflict with an exhorter because of these weaknesses? Please note some

examples and try to identify some of the emotions you felt.

3. Can knowing their gift help you to build or strengthen a spirit-to-spirit relationship with them? How?

4. Can you see why knowing YOUR gift will help you to see how and why they relate to you in the way they do?

5. What could God be trying to teach you through their gifting?

THE GIVER

Giver: (gi -vĕr) one who produces, supplies, grants, offers.

- If you have a deep conviction to raise money to help causes, you might have the gift of giving.
- If you have an excellent business mind and are quite concerned about other's financial needs, you might have the gift of giving.
- If you love to give the big money, but sometimes, deep down, you hope they name a building after you, you might have the gift of giving.
- If you'd rather support a project than lead a project, you might have the gift of giving.
- If you feel strongly that your gift should always be of the highest quality possible, you might have the gift of giving.

Many people have learned to be very generous and even love to give, but there are some people who are uniquely and innately gifted and highly motivated to impart financial and material blessings on others. It compels them. It stimulates them. It's what gets them going in the morning.

You've heard the expression that a person "fell into a compost heap and came out smelling like a rose." That's often the case with the person who has the gift of giving. They seem to be in the right place at the right time. Their investments and business ventures always seem to go well.

Others, however, try to follow their example but never seem to have the same positive experience. Timing, good fortune, keen business sense, excellent foresight . . . people who have been endowed with the gift of giving always seem to have a knack for coming out on top and blessing others.

A Giver's Strengths . . .

- A great desire to see God's causes advanced
- Financial keenness
- Business mind (often respected in the community)
- Personal needs are secondary to other causes
- Often intercedes in prayer for those in need

A Giver's Weaknesses . . .

- Pride in the gift given (enjoys photo opportunities and her name on plaques)
- Builds personal power through the giving of gifts
- Determines spiritual levels in others according to their wealth
- Motivated to meet the needs of others before considering what God wants to accomplish
- Feels rejected when gift is not received

Things a Giver Might Say . . .

If you were to follow a giver around and eavesdrop on some conversations, you might hear comments similar to the following:

- "I felt led to give this to you."
- "It all belongs to the Lord, anyway!"
- "It might make more financial sense if you . . . "
- "Don't worry about the money, Pastor; we'll get it done!"
- "Well, it was just burning a hole in my pocket, anyway!"

Giver Last Seen . . .

If you're on the lookout, here's where you might commonly find someone with the gift of giving:

- Listed on the "Special Thanks" page of any charity's literature
- On the board of a church or ministry
- At philanthropist luncheons
- The VIP window at the bank
- Taking a needy person on a shopping spree

Rest Stop

1. By observing the behavior and attitudes of the people in your life, who would you say might have the gift of giving? What three characteristics come to mind first that might reveal this to you? List them below.

2. Notice the weaknesses of the giver. Have you experienced any conflict with a giver because of

these weaknesses? Please note some examples and try to identify some of the emotions you felt.

3. Can knowing their gift help you to build or strengthen a spirit-to-spirit relationship with them? How?

4. Can you see why knowing YOUR gift will help you to see how and why they relate to you in the way they do?

5. What could God be trying to teach you through their gifting?

THE ADMINISTRATOR

Administrator: (ed -min´ - ə -strā -tẽr) n. one who leads, manages, directs, organizes.

- If you see problems clearly in advance and love devising plans for others to follow, you might have the gift of administration.
- If you're extremely creative and innovative about accomplishing tasks, yet have trouble relaxing until your "To-do" list is done, you might have the gift of administration.
- If you're extremely organized and get things done fast, but sometimes step on others to do it, you might have the gift of administration.

If you need help or accountability with goal-setting or planning a strategy, an administrator is the person you should call. Every exhorter needs to have an administrator close by! They're the ones who make sure we follow through on our abundance of promises. They get the job done, and they get it done now. To them, it's very simple. They just naturally see what needs to be done. They create a schedule. They do it. It's that simple. A little hint, though: Don't mess with their schedule!

I have a good friend who keeps me organized and often travels with me. She had been working extremely hard on some projects, so while we were on the road together, I wanted to stop in a store and buy her a special gift I had in mind. I wanted her to know how much I appreciated her, but she just snapped at me, "There will be no stopping! It's not on the itinerary! If you wanted to plan something special for me, you should have told me yesterday; I would have scheduled it in!"

She sometimes drives me nuts! I wanted to have fun and be spontaneous and thoughtful, but she pulled out her ruler, so to speak, and whacked me on the knuckles! I'll tell you right now, if I weren't aware of (and in need of) her special administrative giftedness, I would have locked her away long ago inside that color-coded, highly-organized, catalogued-by-subject, filing cabinet of hers. She'd probably get out, though. I think that she keeps a spare key filed under *K*.

An Administrator's Strengths . . .

- Sees problems clearly in advance
- Very orderly closets, kitchens, garages
- "Let me give you a list to 'help you'"
- Accomplishes duties quickly (just to get them out of the way)
- Visualizes long-range accomplishments
- Coordinates manpower effectively
- Good at climbing the corporate ladder (companies see great benefit)
- Creative and innovative ways to accomplish tasks

124

An Administrator's Weaknesses . . .

- Can become power-hungry through pride
- Insensitive to others personal desires if they conflict with their own
- "It's only 5:00 P.M., and you want to quit now?"
- Will work excessively to accomplish a task
- Can cause others to feel regimented and unloved

Things an Administrator Might Say . . .

If you were to follow an administrator around and eavesdrop on some conversations, you might hear comments similar to the following:

- "How soon can you have this done?"
- "There's plenty of time in a day if you're organized."
- "How did this place get so cluttered?"
- "If you had listened to me, this never would have happened."
- "Look what time it is, Johnny! You have to get control of your schedule!"

Administrator Last Seen . . .

If you're on the lookout, here's where you might commonly find someone with the gift of administration:

- Climbing the corporate ladder
- An officer in the military
- Meeting planner
- Wedding coordinator
- Store or office manager
- School and hospital administration
- Organizing other people's lives

....
Rest Stop

1. By observing the behavior and attitudes of the people in your life, who would you say might have the gift of administration? What three characteristics come to mind first that might reveal this to you? List them below.

2. Notice the weaknesses of the administrator. Have you been hurt (your spirit bruised) because of an administrator with these weaknesses? (Perhaps they seemed bossy or unloving.) Please note some examples and try to identify some of the emotions you felt.

3. Can knowing their gift help you to build or strengthen a spirit-to-spirit relationship with them? How?

4. Can you see why knowing YOUR gift will help you to see how and why they relate to you in the way they do?

5. What could God be trying to teach you through their gifting?

MERCY

Mercy: (mŭr´ -sē) n. one who feels compassion, extends

help, kindness and forgiveness.

- If you feel the pain of others so much that it affects your mood, you might have the gift of mercy.
- If you'd rather skip lunch and stay after church to counsel a hurting stranger, you might have the gift of mercy.
- If you have irrational fears and are suspicious of everything and everybody, you might have the gift of mercy.
- If, as a child, you brought home all the stray animals or kids, you might have the gift of mercy.

We don't realize how many things we do out of natural reflex. We shiver when we're cold. We yawn when we're tired. Our pulse races when we're scared. We snatch our hand away when something is hot. We duck when someone yells, "Look out!" These are all reflexes, built into our bodies for protection. They're a part of our nervous system and circulatory system.

So too the body of Christ has a set of nerves that are naturally sensitive and watchfully alert to her surroundings. The person with the gift of mercy (or compassion) is uniquely gifted to feel. This role in the body of Christ is critical for the health and harmony of all the members.

Mercy Strengths . . .

- Very considerate of other's feelings
- Able to visualize causes and effects on other's emotions
- Excellent memory for special dates of occasions and personal preferences
- Alert to areas of social injustice
- Able to remain in silence in the background while others receive the glory

- Attracted to those who are misfits or underdogs

Mercy Weaknesses . . .

- Irrational fears projected (with no external basis)
- Assumes negative motives in others (looks for the hidden agenda)
- Fear of rejection may cause violation of conviction (distance themselves from conflict)
- Closes spirit to those she feels are insensitive
- Has a poor self-image (naturally puts herself down so it doesn't hurt so bad when others do)
- Calculating vengeance when wounded comes naturally

Things a Person With the Gift of Mercy Might Say . . .

If you were to follow someone with the gift of mercy around and eavesdrop on some conversations, you might hear comments similar to the following:

- "Oh, I'm so sorry!"
- "I've been praying for you."
- "Can you imagine that?"
- "I can't wait to see how they take that."
- "Are you sure?"

Mercy Last Seen . . .

If you're on the lookout, here's where you might commonly find someone with the gift of mercy:

- Working behind the scenes of any crisis ministry
- On the phone, counseling
- Reading (or writing) a devotional book
- As a nurse in a hospital or home-care environment
- Interceding in prayer for the hurting

....
Rest Stop

1. By observing the behavior and attitudes of the people in your life, who would you say might have the gift of mercy? What three characteristics come to mind first that might reveal this to you? List them below.

2. Notice the weaknesses of the mercy person. Have you experienced any conflict with someone who has these weaknesses? Please note some examples and try to identify some of the emotions you felt.

3. Can knowing their gift help you to build or strengthen a spirit-to-spirit relationship with them? How?

4. Can you see why knowing YOUR gift will help you to see how and why they relate to you in the way they do?

5. What could God be trying to teach you through their gifting?

Just as each of us has one body with many members, and these members do not all have the same function, so in Christ we who are many form one body, and each member belongs to all the others.

—ROMANS 12:4–5

One of the most important keys to walking in excellence is in recognizing our unity as a body of Christ. We are all different, yet we are "one." What an exciting and liberating concept!

Can you imagine what we could accomplish if we all recognized and used our gifts to serve each other? No one would be left in need! Isn't it wonderful being a part of the body of Christ and being supernaturally gifted by God to be used by Him in your own special way?

10

Relating Along the Way

We live with imperfect people in an imperfect world. Sharing the Path of Excellence with others can be extremely challenging, because people can be very difficult to love. While we are all so different in our views, gifts, and ways, we do have one thing in common—our need for each other's love and acceptance. Sometimes, it seems like we can't live with each other, but we know we can't live without each other, either. I've heard many Christians say, "I love the ministry; I just don't like the people."

Some of us feel we could be the perfect mother if only we had that perfect child, or we could be perfect wives if we had perfect husbands. The truth is, we walk with imperfect people . . . just like us.

Have you ever thought about the fact that even if you don't like someone here on earth, you might as well be nice to them because you might be neighbors in heaven? I always make sure I'm *extra nice* to people I don't enjoy being around here on earth. I figure hopefully that God will have their mansion in heaven built on the other side of the crystal sea from me! To be emotionally healthy, we need to learn how to get along with each other. God gave us the Golden Rule of relationships thousands of years ago: "Do unto others as you would have them do unto you." (See Matthew 7:12.) If every one of us would live by this rule, we would live in harmony. As you walk along the path—with those you do like and those you don't—strive for excellence in your relationships by following the principles given below.

RESPECT EACH OTHER'S DIFFERENCES

We are all different by design, and we waste a lot of time and energy trying to change others to be like us. Think about it—do you really want to live in a world where all the people are just like you? I certainly don't. Besides, if two people agree on everything, there is only need for one of them! The Bible says, "As iron sharpens iron, so one man sharpens another" (Prov. 27:17). We are all different, and we need to learn to appreciate and respect those differences.

CREATE COMMON GROUND

"If it is possible, as far as it depends on you, live at peace with everyone" (Rom. 12:18). The fact that someone does not agree with your point of view does not mean they are not worthy of your love and respect.

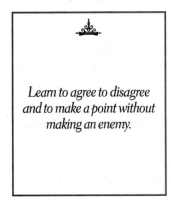

Learn to agree to disagree and to make a point without making an enemy.

Relationships are fragile and too valuable to throw away because of a difference or a disagreement. It's not worth winning the battle and losing the war. Do your best to create common ground.

GIVE OTHERS FREEDOM TO FAIL

The greatest gift you can give someone is the freedom to fail.

Remember, anyone will stay around when all is well. It takes a very special someone to hang in there when things get tough. Many have missed out on the blessing of a long-term friendship because, when someone fails them, they feel the need to move on to the next imperfect person.

Many of us want to bail out of our marriages because our husbands have failed us. But even if we trade in our old one after the romance wears off and he's let us down, new or old, we're still stuck with a man—and an imperfect one at that! And he's stuck with an imperfect woman!

When I first started speaking, I noticed that certain people started putting me up on a pedestal. At first, I enjoyed being looked up to by others. Soon I discovered this was not a blessing at all, because people often assumed I had a "perfect little life."

Unfortunately, the first thing that happened when I failed was that these people took the first exit out of my life that they could find! I felt abandoned. (I'm so thankful that Jesus is the kind of friend who walks in when the world walks out!)

Today, I try to let people know up front that I am human and will make mistakes; I will fail. Hopefully, my failure won't hurt them—it is painful when God has to teach me a lesson at someone else's expense.

> Be humble and gentle. Be patient with each other, making allowance for each other's faults because of your love.
>
> —EPHESIANS 4:2, NLT

Have you ever thought about the fact that *every* great hero of the Bible had flaws and failures? Take heart, at least your failures weren't written up in the best-selling book of all time!

- *Moses* was a man of many excuses. In the presence of God he insisted that he wasn't the man for the job and that God should find someone else!

- *Samson* was known for his incredible physical strength and his one fatal weakness: He fell victim to his pursuit of and slavery to the sensual. He abandoned it all in the fleeting moments of passion.

- *King David* was the most beloved king of all time, but his royal report card is full of bad marks! Not only did he covet his neighbor's wife—he then committed adultery and even tried to hide his sinfulness with murder! Three commandments broken, just like that!

- *Solomon* was the richest and wisest king who ever lived. Yet, despite his wisdom, he spent vast resources and wasted energy on the pursuit of sensual pleasures! The discoveries he made on his journey to take hold of whatever pleased his eye are chronicled in the Book of Ecclesiastes. In the end, as his heart began to turn from his Creator, he found that his selfish pursuits were all vanity and "chasing after the wind."

So what can we learn from the mistakes of those before us? They (and many others) were used greatly by God, *not because they were perfect, but because of God's mercy!* Failure is not final when we let God teach us through our weakness that we need Him. Moses became the most humble man who ever lived. Samson paid the consequences for his weakness, but he was used mightily by God at the end of his life. King David fell to his knees before God and "acknowledged his sin." His repentance didn't do away with the tragic consequences of sin, but he was restored to God and proven to be "a man after God's own heart." Although Solomon rose to greatness in wisdom and wealth, then spiraled slowly into a dark pit of selfish pursuits and compromise, he was still used by God to teach the generations that followed what he learned from his successes and failures.

The Bible also gives us an example of how we are to respond to the failures of others. Galatians 6:1 says, "Brother, if someone is caught in sin, you who are spiritual should restore him gently."

It doesn't say . . .

- Announce his failures to the world.
- Gossip about him at the dinner table.
- Run from him because he failed.
- Give him disapproving looks at church.

If you fell into the snare of sin, how would you want others to react to you? Many times in the church, we hurt our wounded rather than help restore them to the faith. Be careful how harshly you treat others when they fail, because you will be judged by God *with the same attitude that you use to judge others!*

You have a choice. You can react in judgment or with discernment. The difference between the two is attitude— one criticizes, the other cares. Romans 2:1 says, "You, therefore, have no excuse, you who pass judgment on someone else, for at whatever point you judge the other, you are condemning yourself, because you who pass judgment do the same things."

Remember, we're on the same team, fighting the same enemy! Stand in the gap for someone when they fail—pray, encourage, and restore by using the truth in love. First Corinthians 13 says that if we love someone, we will be loyal to him no matter what the cost. We will always believe in him, always expect the best of him, and always stand our ground in defending him. Remember, a house divided against itself will not stand . . . neither will a church . . . or a home.

Tame Your Tongue

The power of life and death is in the tongue. The tongue

can corrupt the whole body. With it we praise our Lord and yet curse our brothers. And even though it is small . . . it makes great boasts. According to the Bible, the tongue is the hardest thing in all the world to control! (See James 3.)

Can you relate? I've learned it's better to swallow my words *before* they come out than to have to eat them later! Unfortunately, most of us talk *first*—then think about what we said after the words are already out there. Think about all of the problems that could be avoided if we could just control our tongues!

> The tongue of the wise brings healing.
> —PROVERBS 12:18

My greatest gift is conversation—my mouth—and I love to use it to motivate and encourage others. But I also recognize that as quickly as I build someone up, I can tear them down. Many times, it happens without my even knowing it.

Never is the tongue more deadly than when we gossip— sharing information, whether it is truthful or not, that hurts someone's reputation. There is an especially deadly force at work in the church that I call "godly gossip." It wounds terribly, yet it is thinly disguised in a cloak of compassion and concern. You may have heard comments like these from a "godly grapevine" in the dark corners of your church:

"Have you heard about Laura? We really need to pray for her. Believe it or not, I heard . . . "

"Now, don't mention this to anyone . . . I'm only telling you this because you're such a prayer warrior . . . "

"I'm not one to gossip, but I think you just need to know this . . . "

"Can you believe what those ladies are saying about Lisa? It's wrong, and that's why I've told the choir ladies . . . "

This kind of "godly gossip" breaks God's heart because we spread the wickedness in His name.

There is another kind of gossip I call "general gossip" that occurs when we gossip about people, churches, ministries, or organizations we don't know personally. We think, *What's the big deal? They don't know me. What can it hurt?* How does it honor God to share the painful mistakes and poor choices others have made? *Unless we are part of the problem or the solution, our concern should always be to build up the body of Christ, whether we know them personally or not!*

A third type of gossip, equally as deadly and easy to fall into, is "silent gossip." When you are standing in a group of gossips and *participate with your ears,* you are participating in the gossip!

At one time a friend was very closely connected with one of my favorite Christian artists. I heard tons of "dirt" about this individual, and it affected me deeply—even though I never said a thing. I realize now that I was just as guilty of gossip as my loose-lipped friend, and, looking back, I wish I had never been a part of this sin of "silence."

Before we speak about others, we need to ask ourselves the following:

1. *Why am I sharing this information?*
2. *Will it hurt someone's reputation?*
3. *Will it benefit the person listening?*
4. *Am I willing to let others use my name as a reference?*
5. *If God were visibly present here with us, would we continue?*

A final warning about gossip: If you have people in your life who gossip *to you,* you can bet that when you're not around they will gossip *about you!* Use your words to build up each other. Remember: Words should minister grace to those who hear. (See Ephesians 4:29.)

WALK WITH CHARACTER AND CREDIBILITY

It is truly an awesome thing to know a person of impeccable

character. They are comfortable to be around because you trust them. They are honest; you can count on their word being truthful and edifying. They are reliable; they let their *yes* be *yes,* and they don't make promises they can't keep. They are committed; they are living out God's call to excellence in their life. The world needs to see spiritual excellence in action—walk with character and credibility in your life.

WALKING IN UNITY AND LOVE

If a doctor were asked to describe in one word what it means to have ultimate physical health, I'm sure his answer would have to be *unity*—every cell working harmoniously together exactly as it should; each bringing in nourishment, releasing energy, and getting rid of toxins. Although each cell is unique in design and function, there is a perfect working relationship when there is perfect unity. Where there is perfect unity, there is perfect health.

The same can be said for our spiritual health. Where we find perfect unity, we will find a healthy Spirit-to-spirit relationship. The ultimate example of this is the relationship between God the Father and Jesus Christ the Son. This is our pattern for spiritual excellence because it shows the perfect unity between the Father and the Son that existed from the beginning of time.

In Jesus' final agony-filled prayer in the garden before His arrest, He told the Father, "I have given them the glory that you gave me, that they may be one as we are one. I in them and you in me. May they be brought to complete unity to let the world know that you sent me and have loved them even as you have loved me" (John 17:22–23).

God sees us as individuals; He loves us passionately because He made us. He also wants us to be "one" so that we can be a reflection of the divine unity between God the Father and Jesus the Son. What makes this unity possible? What connects us and holds us together in spite of our differences?

Love is patient and kind. Love is not jealous or boastful or proud or rude. Love does not demand its own way. Love is not irritable, and it keeps no record of when it has been wronged. It is never glad about injustice but rejoices whenever the truth wins out. Love never gives up, never loses faith, is always hopeful, and endures through every circumstance.

—1 CORINTHIANS 13:4–7, NLT

Love is the *spiritual glue* that connects us. Love is *the reason God made us* and *the reason He sent His Son to redeem us.* Love is also the *fruit (the evidence) of God living inside us.* People will know we belong to Him because of our love. This love is not a superficial love that we see so commonly around us, but it is God's definition of love . . . *a spiritual love.*

We can know many people and still feel very lonely in this world, in the church, or even in a marriage. Loneliness is cured when we learn to develop spirit-to-spirit relationships with each other.

A spiritual friend . . .

- Knows my feelings.
- Reveals to me how she feels.
- Teaches me about myself.
- Is comfortable with silence.
- Feels free to tell me the truth.
- Gives me freedom to fail.
- Loves me for who I am.

A superficial friend . . .

- Only knows the facts about me.
- Tells me what she's done.
- Tells me about others.
- Feels awkward with silence.

- Would leave me if I let her down.
- Loves me for what I can do.

....
Rest Stop

1. Take a look at some healthy relationships in your life. What makes them healthy?

2. What are the principles for establishing excellence in relationships in which you excel?

3. Which principles do you have a difficult time with and need to work on?

11

Spirit-to-Spirit Marriages

As we examine some of the relationships that we form on this Path of Excellence, far too many of us—if we're honest—must list our marriages among those that have suffered casualties. Marriage is supposed to be the pinnacle of earthly relationships—the closest union two people can make in the site of God and mankind. But because of this special place in God's design, marriage can also be the home of the greatest heartache and pain. That is why, if you are married, the biggest contributing factor to your emotional health is your relationship with your husband. He can be an instrument used by God for healing, or he can be the cause of great insecurity and pain.

For years, I couldn't figure out why I was so depressed and lonely in my own marriage. Our marriage was picture-perfect on the outside . . . good enough to hang on the walls of the "great-looking marriage" museum.

My husband, Steve, and I traveled and ministered together. He loved the Lord and was a devoted and loving father. But I was still hurting. Behind the "image" of the healthy marriage, I was dying inside.

I had a craving for value and acceptance from Steve, but he seemed more concerned about keeping up appearances than understanding my heart or feeling my pain. I was already an expert at denial, so my natural response was to put on a happy face and play the "I'm-so-happily-married" game. As I look back, I know that this was the wrong thing to do with my pain. Once again, I learned the hard way that if you don't deal with your pain, it will deal with you. We became so good at pretending, that my husband didn't have a clue about how much emotional pain I was in. He didn't know how to recognize all the warning signs:

- My weekly crying spells (he thought I was just emotional or had PMS).
- My deteriorating health (he thought he'd better help me more with my diet).
- My semiannual habit of exchanging all our furniture for something else, something different (he thought I just loved change).

What I really needed from Steve was to feel loved, valued, accepted, and appreciated as a person. Though occasionally he could say the words, we really didn't have a spirit-to-spirit relationship. I continued to pull away emotionally. I just had to protect my heart from more pain. He continued on with "life as usual."

By stuffing my pain, I forced other things to resurface. I slowly began drifting back into the eating disorder bondage that I thought I had been delivered from. I felt so ungodly for the way I was feeling. *Why am I so emotional and over-sensitive? Why does my husband affect me the way he does? Please, God! I beg you! Take away these feelings!*

But God wouldn't take the feelings away. Instead, He taught me a remarkable truth: That my longing for intimacy and my craving for value and acceptance from Steve was by His design! It was how He made me to be!

No other relationships have this dynamic potential for spirit-to-spirit intimacy—or rejection. Our husbands have the power to crush our spirit like no one else can. With this power comes great responsibility for the husband to care for his wife and live with her in an understanding way—as Christ would. (See 1 Peter 3:7.) *But even the most dedicated of men have trouble understanding the incredible power they have to make or break us!*

Lyndi McCartney, wife of Coach Bill McCartney, was emotionally bruised and neglected for more than thirty years while her husband was "sold out" to coaching football and then to Promise Keepers, the men's ministry he founded. She was so depressed that she lost over eighty pounds as she threw up her food every single day for seven months. After Christian counseling, Bill finally looked at his wife's despair and emotional pain and decided to face the evidence. His conclusion was simple and profound. "I had caused this!" he wrote. "Lyndi's depression was the toxic fallout from a vast legacy of my chronic insensitivity and neglect toward her. Her emotional defenses had been beaten down through years of wanting, of waiting."[1]

Sadly, according to Lyndi, despite all the warnings she had given him, it wasn't until she stopped being supportive of him that he finally began to notice. He started noticing her pain but felt lost about what to do. His heart was finally pierced by a powerful statement he heard from a preacher who said, "If you really want to know the character of a man, look into the face of his wife. Whatever he has invested in or withheld from her will be reflected in her countenance." When Bill looked squarely at his wife's face, his heart sank. "What I saw stunned me. Her face was sad and empty. Her eyes, once so bright and effervescent, had lost their sparkle. I saw pain . . . slow decay . . . emotional torment . . . she appeared drained, depleted, and unfulfilled. What had I done?"[2]

Often as wives, we try to hide our feelings. We feel guilty for feeling them, and we don't want to burden our husbands.

But the truth is that we just cannot help being affected by them. Like a radar, God made our spirits sensitive to our husband's words—spoken and unspoken. Sensitive to his motives—good and bad. Sensitive to his spirit—proud or humble. Sensitive to his attitudes toward us—hidden or open.

If we do succeed, for a time, in covering up the effect our husband is having on us, we are doing more than deceiving ourselves. We are contributing to his ignorance concerning matters of the heart! By *not* drawing attention to the effect he is having on our spirit, we endorse his blindness. We are his means of developing his awareness of spirit-to-spirit relationships! By remaining silent we lose, and he remains ignorant to his own spirit and to the hurts and needs of others around him. If this continues, we will eventually close up our heart for protection, and he will lose his spiritual gauge—his radar—forever.

CONSIDER THIS PRINCIPLE

Our ability to have healthy spirit-to-spirit relationships with each other is evidence of our capacity to have a healthy Spirit-to-spirit relationship with God!

> Husbands, love your wives, just as Christ loved the church and gave himself up for her to make her holy, cleansing her by the washing with water through the word, and to present her to himself as a radiant church, without stain or wrinkle or any other blemish, but holy and blameless. In this same way, husbands ought to love their wives as their own bodies.
> —EPHESIANS 5:25–28

The turning point in our marriage came when we finally listened to a friend and scheduled an appointment with Ken Nair of Life Partners Christian Ministries. His nationwide "Discovery Seminar" revealed insights from the Scriptures and opened up amazing new understanding regarding our relationship with God, each other, and others. Through their intensive, three-year Christ-Quest Institute, we've experienced hope and healing through the power of God's Word and by better understanding each other's spirit.

I was excited to learn that my emotions are not something I need to deny, hide, or feel guilty about having! Because emotions are designed by God to reveal the condition of our spirit, we can look honestly at our feelings as an expression—or indicator—of what's going on inside. It's the first step toward having a healthy spirit-to-spirit relationship.

It's okay to feel! God made us that way. And it's okay to express those feelings to each other in a context of love. Steve is now learning to listen to and understand my spirit—not just my words. This is an extremely difficult task for most men. They naturally *think facts* instead of *feeling hurts*. They often respond mechanically instead of emotionally. One of Ken's principles is: "When it comes to a man perceiving and understanding his wife's spirit, women have no idea of the depth of the ignorance they are wrestling with!"

Women often say, "My husband stuffs his feelings!" Through Ken, however, we learned, "No, ma'am, he has to recognize his feelings before he can stuff them." My husband now realizes this and agrees, but for years his complaint was that I didn't understand him. After all, if I understood what he really meant, I would not be so wounded by his words! That never helped either of us. I still hurt. Like stepping on someone's foot—whether on purpose or by accident—it still has painful consequences. I, likewise, am understanding more about my role as a helper. I also am appreciating the incredible responsibility God has given to a husband to care for his wife—not only by understanding her, but also by ministering to her spirit through affirmation and nurturing in order for her to flourish in the role that God has her.

In the Garden of Eden, when God looked upon all of His creation—the splendor of all He had made—He noticed something that wasn't good. It wasn't man's form or his mind or even his physical ability; it was his "aloneness."

Alone? Adam wasn't alone, was he? He was fellowshiping with God Himself! Adam could spend time with God every day in the garden. Could it be that God pulled back the curtain of Adam's tomorrow and saw that his coming rebellion would sever the special relationship that he had with God? God saw man's future need. He then did something He had never done before. He caused Adam to fall into a deep sleep and took a rib from his side. From it, He fashioned woman. God didn't make her from the dust of the ground or speak her into existence like He did the rest of creation. He formed her from the side of man. Bone of his bone, flesh of his flesh. A helper suitable for his needs "after the fall" . . . when Spirit-to-spirit fellowship with God was lost.

So what did God see in man that he needed "help" with? You may be surprised. We can get interesting insights from ancient Hebrew—the language of the earliest Old Testament writers. Ancient Hebrew, as in most ancient languages, used written symbols to communicate. These symbols then became letters as the language developed. The word that we now translate as *helper* had three letters from the Hebrew alphabet. These letters in ancient Hebrew were the symbols for "see or reveal," "axe," and "man." When you combine the last two symbols, you get "ax man," which can be translated "enemy" (the Hebrew word is *czar*). So, when you put it all together, the word for *helper* really is translated "revealer of the enemy."

This is profound and encouraging news for women who are frustrated with husbands who just don't "get it!" God created us with the unique capacity to be supersensitive relationally and more "in tune" emotionally than our husbands. Men can be bonded to other men and attached to their dogs and their cars, but why do they have so much trouble with heart-to-heart relationships with their wives?

A man's wife is the God-given person in his life given the function to naturally, involuntarily reveal his enemy—*his flesh!* There is nothing more stubborn than the flesh. It absolutely refuses to die willingly, so men react to women for doing the job given to them by God.

A term for this God-given role for the wife is "a spiritual gauge" for her husband. As a man is controlled by his flesh, he will reject her unique sensitivity and will neglect her needs as a fragile, "weaker" vessel. The wife then builds walls behind which she can withdraw emotionally, and her husband, ignorant of it all, loses the spiritual gauge that his wife was created to be. Sadly, he also loses his chance for real intimacy and a deep spirit-to-spirit relationship.

The results can be tragic, as we see in countless unfulfilled marriages—even among Christians. The counselor who sat across the desk from Bill McCartney recognized that, despite his credentials as a tough-guy coach and Christian leader, when it came to dying to the flesh and healing the emotional wounds he had inflicted on his wife, this would be the toughest fight of his life.

However, if a man is willing to do what it takes to be Christlike, to take responsibility for his wife's emotional health, and to minister to her spirit, there can be a fulfilling "happily-ever-after" relationship. Coach McCartney and his wife, Lyndi, as well as my husband, Steve, and I, are now seeing true victory in our marriages for that very reason.

If you're struggling in your marriage and lack the intimacy and emotional healing that you need, take heart in knowing that Jesus suffered rejection and abandonment from those closest to Him. He also never gave up. If you are not constructively honest with your husband, he may never know how he is affecting you. If you say everything is fine, or act like that is the case, don't be surprised if he takes you at face value and does nothing to fix that which is "fine." If he doesn't care or believe you when you are honest with him, that doesn't mean you must be wrong or that God doesn't love you. Since you crave his acceptance, it will be natural to blame yourself or agree with him when, or if, he blames his failure to care for your spirit (as Christ would care for it) on you. Don't accept that blame.

You cannot change your husband! In fact, changing him is

not your job. *Your job is to help him accomplish the task of changing himself!* You cannot help God by being silent if you see what your husband does not see. God is with you. He still has great plans for you even in the midst of your storm.

••••••••••••••••••••••••••
Rest Stop

1. If you're married, have you noticed that you don't have a spirit-to-spirit relationship? What indicators reveal that to you?

2. Can you recall issues that have never been resolved? What emotional effect did they have on you?

3. Do you spend more time talking to friends than you do with your husband? Why? What about? Can you identify why you don't share your heart with him?

4. If you have a husband who is willing to be like Christ with you, what would be changed in your marriage?

Note: Some of this information just scratches the surface on the important issue of spirit-to-spirit marriages. For more study, contact Life Partners Christian Ministries at (800) 685–7257, extension 6731.

1. Bill McCartney with David Halbrook, *Sold Out: Becoming Man Enough to Make a Difference* (Nashville, TN: Word Publishing, 1997), 230.
2. Ibid.

12

Following Your Calling

All my life I wanted to be a princess. My mom was a beauty queen, and my dad was a disc jockey in Hollywood who hosted beauty pageants. I was in awe of the sparkling crown. Once when I was a little girl, I was backstage with my dad while he was hosting a pageant. The crown was sitting on a table in the dark. I tugged at my dad's hand, "Daddy, why doesn't the crown sparkle?"

"Well, Rosie," he responded, "a crown can only sparkle when a light shines through it."

The same is true of us. We only sparkle when the light of Jesus shines through our lives, our words, our actions, and our eyes. Even if we perfect ourselves physically and emotionally, without spiritual beauty, especially to others, our lives look dull.

When I won the crown of Mrs. USA in 1994, my son, Jacob, was in kindergarten. He couldn't wait to go to school and share his mommy's victory at show-and-tell time. With eyes beaming, he ran into class and yelled, "Guess what, everybody! My mommy is the new queen of the country!"

149

That day, when I came to pick up Jacob at school, I certainly did not look like a queen. I had on no makeup, my hair was in a bun, and I was wearing an oversized gray sweat suit. I was worn out from a weekend of speaking, and I'm one of those women who, when I don't wear makeup, don't have a face! When I got there, Jacob's teacher pulled me aside with a big smile and exclaimed, "Your little boy loves you so much that he actually thinks you're Mrs. USA!"

I said, "I am!"

She looked me over and shot back with an incredulous smirk, "You're kidding!" She was surprised because my appearance and actions didn't match up with her "beauty queen" expectations. I certainly didn't "look" like Mrs. USA!

Even though this story is funny, it's not so humorous when someone looks at us and sees the way we act or talk and says, "You're kidding! You're a Christian? You're a daughter of the King?"

THE ROYAL CALL

The truth is, we *are* royalty. We have a crown, and that crown is eternal. We have a banner, and that banner is love. We have a reign here on earth, and that reign is temporary. The Bible says we did not choose God, but rather *He chose us!* There is a royal call on our lives. We were set apart for a special purpose. (See 1 Peter 2:9.)

The first step to living out this royal call is to recognize our God-appointed position. Our God is King above all kings. He loves us so much that He wants to give us peace, power, purpose, and position in His Kingdom! If that doesn't make you feel special, I don't know anything that will!

He created a program to teach us how to walk, talk, act, and look like a daughter of the King. In God's Holy Word, these incredible words of wisdom, truth, and love will give us supernatural power—a power we can call on anytime by praying in the name of Jesus and that will give us the strength to go through His royal preparation.

ROYAL PREPARATION

The royal preparation is designed to strengthen your character so you will be ready to handle the attacks of the enemy—an enemy who wants to destroy God's kingdom. Every mighty man or woman of God has gone through this preparation. Without it, they would not have been equipped to live out their royal call!

The call is not about *comfort;* it's about *character.* David was in a cave during his preparation for his royal call. Joseph was in a prison during his preparation. Queen Esther's preparation gave her the courage to risk her life to save her people. The purpose of this call is not about pain; it's about power. It's not about trials; it's about triumph. Great battles bring great victory.

Several years ago, God moved my heart to help those with hidden pain. Sometimes I would feel their pain so deeply that I would weep uncontrollably. Because of the royal preparation God allowed me to go through, I knew in my spirit that there were millions who carried pain no one could see on the outside. I wanted to be used to help them unveil that pain so they could have victory in their life.

Through praying, God revealed to me the Fit for Excellence ministry. I was as excited as a pregnant woman who couldn't wait to see her baby! As I began to take the necessary steps for this deliverance ministry, I had no idea how hard the labor pains would be. Today, I can honestly say that this royal call has been worth every trial, every pain, and every tear I've had to cry to see thousands of women discover God's call to the Path of Excellence in their lives.

All of us are in preparation for a royal call. In fact, God has an incredible call on your life. The question is, "Will you answer it?"

LIVING OUT THE CALL

To live out the royal call God has on your life, you will have to be willing to walk away from some things in the world. What you are willing to walk away from will determine how much God can bring to you.

Jesus said, "Anyone who is only interested in this life will end up losing their eternal life, but the person who is willing to give up everything and follow Me will be happy in this life and will also be given eternal life." (See Matthew 16:25.)

The most important thing when entering into your calling is "to be faithful with little and He will give you much." If your passion is to teach, become an expert on the ways of God as shown in the Scripture. Start small—in your neighborhood, Sunday school, or with your friends. If your passion is to serve, volunteer at a ministry. If it's to evangelize, let God familiarize you with His Word, then start telling others one-on-one about Jesus. If it's to administrate, help with functions at church or coordinate special events.

Again, don't be afraid to start small. If you try to jump in the Red Sea before God parts it, your dreams may drown, and you'll miss out on God's promises for your life.

Take a moment to write some practical steps you can take to live out your royal call. Pray and ask God to show you if your plans are just a good idea or a God idea. He who started the work in you will be faithful to complete it in you. (See Philippians 1:6.) The best way to enter into the ministry is to get involved where God is already at work (an existing ministry at your church or in your community).

TALKING LIKE ROYALTY

Create a conversation that brings glory to God. Talk about His wonderful works, His miracles, and His grace. Let people know how exciting it is to know Him. Don't gossip about your brothers and sisters in Christ. Don't put your pastor down. That only causes others to stumble and stay away. Jesus turned the water into wine, but He can't turn our "whining" into anything! Talk like a daughter of the King, and you'll feel like one. God's Word says the power of life and death is in our tongue. Talk life!

Living Like Royalty

No matter what surrounds us in the outside world, we can create a beautiful surrounding and a presence of peace in our homes. Living like royalty is not about money; it's about the effort we put into making our home a warm and welcoming environment for people to enter. I don't live in a big beautiful home, and we certainly don't have a lot of money. Even on our limited budget, I've discovered some creative ways to make our home feel more like a castle:

- Play Christian music throughout the day.
- Keep the house in order, and you'll feel in order.
- Use lots of flowers and scented candles.
- Keep big bowls full of fresh fruit.
- Have a comfortable, quiet place in your home where you can read, study, or just relax.
- Write sweet notes to your family or roommates.
- Turn off the TV and talk to each other.
- Light a fire in the fireplace.
- Make a special meal for your family (as you would for guests).

Money can only buy an expensive house. It cannot build a loving home. I've learned that you can always make more money, but you can never buy back time. The most valuable thing in your home is your relationship with each other.

The Kingdom's Call

Once upon a time there was a beautiful, faraway kingdom

of fairy-tale proportions. The king's palace sat majestically upon a grand mountain estate surrounded by crystal lakes and unending brightly colored gardens. At the edge of the king's estate was a dangerous gorge with sharp rocks and menacing cliffs. On the other side of the dangerous gorge was a bustling, industrious town filled with skilled laborers and intelligent workers. The townspeople were known the world over as the best bridge builders in all the land. Every living soul, with the exception of orphans, worked long, hard hours to build the most beautiful bridges the world had ever seen. Bridges were everywhere. Every home was joined together by magnificent bridges—some large, some small. Some were sparkly and ornate with grandly designed pillars and some were simple and practical.

Dignitaries came from far and wide just to see the intricate and spectacular creations. Many foreigners ordered bridges for their own countries, and some bridges even spanned the great distances between the bustling little town and the surrounding villages. Their reputation as master bridge builders was unsurpassed.

Little Sarah was one of the orphans who lived under the large bridge near the edge of town. She had been very sick as an infant, and, as she grew, her strength never quite caught up with her. Because she was unable to work like the rest of the children, she lived on leftovers and scraps from the bridge builders who traveled overhead on their way to and from work.

The superintendent of bridge building was a proud, tough old man who worked his crews mercilessly. Nevertheless, he had taken a liking to little Sarah. He often stopped by the bridge where Sarah lived and gave her an extra sandwich from his lunchbox on his way to work. She knew that he had won many bridge-building awards and certificates of excellence and that he was constantly praised for a lifetime of amazing achievements. Yet, despite the superintendent's stellar reputation, Sarah was not the least bit impressed. She knew he built the best bridges in the world, but no matter how long, or high, or wide, or expensive, or strong, or excellent the bridges were, they never led anywhere really interesting. "Why can't he build a bridge across the gorge to the king's estate?" she wondered.

Every single day for as long as the townspeople could remember, a majestic bell was heard in the distance. In fact, it was so consistent that everyone in all the land would set their clocks by it. It signified the peak of the day, the pinnacle of opportunity. It was known as the Kingdom's Call because, from across the gorge and up the mountain, the king himself would stand in his splendid palace and pull the mighty cord that made the bell ring. Then his son, the prince, would walk down the royal path from the palace, around the crystal lakes, through the flower gardens, all the way down the majestic mountain to the edge of the gorge that surrounded the king's estate. There, at the end of the path, the prince would stand watching and waiting.

As custom tells it, this was a moment for all the townspeople to stop their labor and proudly wave to the prince. The bridge superintendent, like many others, recognized this as an opportunity to stand atop his latest bridge and take a slow bow—eyes gleaming with the pride that comes from great accomplishment. *Perhaps,* he thought, *the prince will tell the king of this, my latest and most excellent creation!*

For many, many years, this custom had become the highlight of the day for the townspeople. In fact, they were so concerned about waving proudly to the prince that they had stopped noticing that there was indeed a bridge that spanned across the gorge! It stretched from the edge of the cliff where the prince stood all the way across the deep chasm to the town's edge. The people never really paid any attention to the bridge, because it wasn't really a bridge after all—not like any the superintendent or anyone else had ever built, anyway. It consisted only of two long ropes stretched precariously between wooden stakes that were pounded into the rocky cliffs on each side. Between the ropes old boards were fastened with rough leather straps.

When Sarah was small, the older kids told her the ancient story of the ugly old bridge and how the king himself had made it before anyone lived on this side. He himself designed and built it, but he sternly warned his subjects that no one was allowed to cross the gorge; if they did, they would die on the other side. Well, two adventurous souls saw the other side as a tremendous opportunity for starting their very own town so, one day long ago, they crossed the dangerous gorge on the old ugly bridge. These two adventurers were the first man and woman, and their rebellious and courageous act put the proud, new, beautiful town on the map.

When Sarah inquired about the ugly old rope bridge and why no one ever dared walk back across to join the prince and the king, the children scoffed at her. "Everyone knows," they laughed with an eerie smirk, "that ugly old thing isn't even a bridge at all! It's the walk of death! Besides, the prince has no intentions of bringing any of us to the other side alive!"

Every day, when the Kingdom Call sounded, Sarah's thoughts wandered toward the direction of the gorge, the ugly old bridge, the prince, and the beautiful kingdom on the other side. It wasn't long until she followed her thoughts and started wandering in that direction herself. Without anyone noticing, she would slip away from under the bridge and hide in the thick, flowered bushes at the edge of the gorge—beckoned by the Kingdom's Call and the sight of the prince. Every day, she would crouch in the bushes directly opposite from where the prince stood. She and her majesty were separated only by the deep chasm and the ugly old bridge. She had never been this close to him and was quite surprised that the other townspeople were not as fascinated by the prince's presence as she was. The royal prince was strong and handsome. His brilliant, purple robe was draped with a dazzling gold sash that danced quietly in the wind. His royal crown seemed to reflect every ray of light from the midday sun and illuminate his face. Sarah could see very clearly his warm, gentle smile and piercing eyes that seemed to call out patiently for someone—anyone—to return his gaze. As she crouched in her hiding place, she could see the townspeople in the distance abruptly stop what they were doing and wave to the prince, as was their custom. Some were bowing atop their well-crafted bridges and others were winking with a self-approving "thumbs up."

For many days Sarah continued watching the Kingdom's Call in this fashion. From her vantage point on the edge of the gorge, she became familiar with the prince's wonderful and expressive face. Interestingly, she noticed that after each Kingdom's Call, before the prince turned to walk alone back up to the palace, his warm smile would disappear. Without fail, before he would turn to go, his gaze would slowly drop from the horizon (where his bridge-building subjects were busily at work) to the gorge that separated them, and then to the ground.

Sarah could tell that something was definitely not right. Each day the prince's smile would vanish as he turned sadly toward the palace.

Perhaps our bridges aren't as pleasing as we thought, Sarah reasoned. *Maybe if he would cross over, he could get a better look at our excellent creations.*

The next morning, when the superintendent stopped by, Sarah asked him about the prince.

"Years ago," the superintendent answered, "when I was young, the prince would cross that ugly old bridge every morning to walk among us. He'd offer to bring us across the gorge with him to live in the palace with the king, but no one was really interested. Pretty soon, he stopped asking. Now, he doesn't even cross the bridge anymore. He just stands there. Some say he's still asking us to join him, but most of us who know better are certain he's just inspecting our grand creations and taking notes on our bridge-building progress."

Sarah could not hide her mounting confusion. "Why in the world has no one ever gone with him?" she questioned boldly. "It's quite obvious that he wants us to!"

The superintendent smiled and patted her on the head. "Don't you know? There is absolutely no need for bridges in the kingdom! All of our excellent creations and hard work are useless over there. That's why no one has taken the risk. We just work until we die and hope our efforts and acclaim will pass inspection and win us favor with the king and a place in his kingdom. Besides, that ugly old bridge is a worthless piece of junk. Our town condemned it years ago."

Sarah was not the least bit satisfied with the superintendent's response. That night, her youthful curiosity kept her awake the entire night. Although the cold, stone bridge offered her little protection from the howl of late-night winds that knifed right through the torn old rags she wore, Sarah had delightful visions of the kingdom and the prince and his bountiful gardens around the crystal lakes. She wanted badly to see what was in the palace and tried with all her imagination to picture the king's glorious face.

The next day, Sarah could hardly wait for the Kingdom's Call. When the bell sounded, she ran from under the bridge as quickly as her frail little body could carry her to the special hiding spot in the thick, flowered bush at the edge of the gorge. As the prince approached, she felt desperately like she wanted to say something to him. She felt her throat tighten and her pulse begin to race. Her gaze was transfixed to his face, and she didn't even pay attention as the townspeople gave their customary wave. Under her breath, safely hidden within the bush, she spoke from the depths of her soul, yet barely a whisper emerged, "Oh, dear prince, why have you come?"

It was then that the most amazing thing happened. The prince's majestic gaze fell directly on the thick, flowered bush where Sarah was hiding! He was looking right at her! Had he heard her heart's whisper? Sarah's chest pounded wildly. She felt for sure the branches were throbbing with her every pulse. Then suddenly, he spoke.

"I've come to be with you, Sarah; don't be afraid."

Sarah gulped. Her shaking knees suddenly stiffened, and the next thing she knew, she had stood to her feet, directly opposite the prince!

He continued gently, "Why have you come, Sarah?"

Sarah just stood there staring at the prince, but then felt her fear melt away. As their eyes locked, she found within her a strange boldness.

"The superintendent says you've just come to inspect our fine bridges," Sarah blurted.

The prince shook his head slowly from side to side and smiled. Sarah squinted as the jewels from his royal crown flickered in the sun, tossing brilliant pieces of light across the gorge and onto her dirty face and dusty brown hair. "Sarah, your town has always built the finest bridges in the land." The prince paused. "Yet, I'm not interested in building bridges, Sarah, if they don't bring us closer together. My father, the king, rings the bell every day to call his people to come to him. I stand here every day, not to inspect bridges, but to search hearts. Hoping someone will want to join us in the kingdom."

Sarah was both thrilled and confused. "But how," she asked, "can we possibly join you, O great prince? Our bridges are useless to cross the deep gorge, and the ugly old bridge is condemned!"

Before she could finish speaking, the prince took a step onto the ugly old bridge. Without even taking his eyes off Sarah, he walked effortlessly across. In a moment's time, he stood in front of her. By now, the townspeople had ceased their customary wave and stood frozen in disbelief as the majestic prince and the orphan Sarah stood together on the edge of the gorge. Sarah didn't even notice them.

The prince placed his hand on Sarah's shoulder and knelt down next to her so that he could look directly in her eyes. "It is true," he began, "that no one can cross the gorge on their own. Yet, I have come to take anyone who would like to join me."

Sarah's eyes brightened. "Take me, Your Majesty!" she pleaded.

With that, the royal prince picked up the small orphan girl into his strong, comforting arms, and, just as surely as he had crossed, he walked to the other side of the dangerous gorge. Not once did he take his eyes off his new friend, Sarah. She trusted his steps and felt so sure of his grip that she never stopped smiling. Once they were safely on the other side, the prince gently placed her on her feet. For the first time since anyone could remember, someone from the village had done something besides waving and bowing at the Kingdom's Call. Someone had actually crawled into the prince's arms and in a few grand, bold, miraculous steps crossed safely across the dangerous gorge on that ugly old bridge to join the royal prince and the mighty king in their glorious kingdom. That someone was a little girl named Sarah.

The townspeople were not quite sure what to do. Some rubbed their eyes in disbelief; others looked around at each other inquisitively. Still others just shrugged their shoulders, shook their heads, and went back to work. That afternoon, bridge-building continued as usual. By the time the warm, red sun drifted lazily to sleep behind the kingdom's farthest mountain peaks, most of the townspeople had forgotten all about the little orphan girl who used to live under the bridge.

Sarah and the prince wasted no time whatsoever at the edge of the gorge. They turned and walked together up the hill, danced through the radiant flower gardens, and skipped across the top of the crystal lake. "Who needs dumb ol' bridges!" Sarah laughed. On they went, up to the palace, where everything was more spectacular than Sarah could have ever imagined. She knew it would take a "forever" of fun to explore the exciting things found in the kingdom. When they arrived at the palace gates, everyone there stopped what they were doing and waved and cheered for Sarah, who was met with a hug by the mighty king. It was there, amid the cheering crowd, that the king knelt down next to Sarah and placed a small golden crown upon her head. He then looked her in the eye and, with a wink, announced proudly, "Welcome home, my princess."

A POWERFUL PRINCESS

Several years ago, I had the privilege of knowing a true princess. Rachel was thirteen years old when she was diagnosed with cancer. She knew she was a daughter of the King, and she did not allow her illness to stop her from living out her royal call. She also knew God could heal her, but she loved her King so much that she said, "I will finish what God has called me to do, even if He doesn't heal me." I'll never forget what she said to me when I called to encourage her. "Sheri, I don't know how much longer I have here on earth, so I need to hurry and tell as many of my classmates as possible about Jesus." She asked her family to pray for her every day, not just for healing, but for a divine appointment. Her pain gave her power.

Every day for three years, this little princess had a divine appointment at her high school. The kids could not understand why Rachel was so concerned about them when *she* was the one dying of cancer. On her sixteenth birthday, she announced, "I'm ready to go home to be with the Lord. I just want to see my high school class in heaven someday."

That night Rachel wrote a letter to her classmates. A few weeks later she went home to be with the Lord. Her final request, before she died, was that her classmates would attend her funeral. Rachel had been such a light in the darkness at her high school that the principal made buses available for the kids to attend her funeral. The pastor read Rachel's final letter to the huge gathering. It said, "Do not mourn for me, for today I am in God's kingdom, where there is no more sickness, no more pain, and no more death. My only prayer is that I would see you again someday on the other side of eternity. My Savior, Jesus Christ, made a way for you to get there." Then the pastor asked the kids, "How many of you want to go to heaven when you die?" Hundreds came forward and gave their lives to Jesus Christ. You see, one little princess with cancer affected hundreds of lives. Just think how many of those young people were changed forever and became godly examples for their families and their communities.

Don't allow painful circumstances to stop you from living out God's royal call on your life.

····························

Rest Stop

1. When you die, what will people remember about you? Will you enter into the eternal kingdom?

BECOMING A DAUGHTER OF THE KING

Every day God is calling us down the path toward eternity. He longs to have a royal relationship with us. He sent the Prince of Peace to make a way for us to enter into His kingdom.

Jesus was in the world, and though the world was made through Him, the world did not recognize Him. He came to that which was His own, but His own did not receive Him. Yet, to all who received Him, to those who believed in His name, He gave the right to become children of God (John 1:10–12).

Becoming a daughter of the King is an incredible honor. This moment was orchestrated in the heavenlies just for you. It is not a coincidence that you are reading this book. God's Word says He went out of His way to choose you. You have the opportunity to accept or reject His offer. Although He loves you, He will not pressure you. It is your decision. Right here, right now, I would like to invite you to receive the greatest crown of all—the eternal crown of life.

Rest Stop

If you have never called on the King, I invite you to pray this simple prayer with me:

Dear God, I have not lived my life in a way that honors You. Please forgive me for my sins and come into my heart. Give me a new life through Your Son, Jesus. I thank You now that my name has been recorded in the Book of Life.

If you said that prayer and meant it with all your heart, and if you believe that Jesus is the Son of the living God, then you are a daughter of the King! The angels in heaven are rejoicing at this very moment!

Now would be a good time to write out a prayer of thanks to God for your new life.

13

Adventures With the King

There's nothing more exciting or fulfilling than going on daily adventures with the King. God's Word says that the steps of a righteous man (or woman) are ordered of the Lord (Ps. 37:23). Did you know that every day your God has an appointment for you to keep? You can, however, miss your divine appointments when you are too busy thinking about your own agenda. If you're not experiencing the joy of your salvation, it may be because you're missing your daily divine appointments!

Divine appointments can happen anywhere—at the gas station, dry cleaners, or grocery store. Just think, the next time you're in the grocery store, standing behind someone who has two hundred coupons to save four dollars, that could be your opportunity to pray them out of "coupon bondage"! Or to give a word of encouragement to the cashier or pray for the people who are waiting behind you in line! Whatever the case, there's always an opportunity to make a difference in someone's life while you are going about your daily routine.

Divine appointments keep us focused on eternity and give us something exciting to talk about—rather than complaining about the things that challenge and frustrate us during the day.

Because I love to shop, my family says I have a "mall ministry." (I try to convince my husband that my ministry would be much more effective if he'd increase the limit on my shopping budget!) I've had some wonderful divine appointments at the mall. One day while I was shopping for makeup with my sisters-in-law, I noticed that the woman working at the counter was in emotional pain. Even though the counter was full of customers, I pulled her aside, asked her if she was okay, and asked if I could pray for her. She immediately burst into tears. She told me how her husband had just had an affair and had left her and the children. She was devastated, and she didn't know the Lord. After I prayed with her, I asked her if my husband and I could come by her house on Sunday and bring her and her children to church. She said she'd never been to church before, but she was hurting so badly that she was willing to try anything. The pastor gave a message on how God is a father to the fatherless and a husband to the husbandless. With tears in her eyes, the woman came forward with her children; they all gave their lives to Jesus Christ.

Every one of us has the opportunity to be God's extended hand of love to someone in need. The key is to look for the divine appointment that God has scheduled for you each day—and not be so consumed with our own agenda that you miss the opportunity to touch a life.

When my husband was in seminary, he was talking with some classmates about their plans for the Christmas holiday break. One particular student was a new pastor from Nigeria who had not seen his family in two years because he couldn't afford the airfare to fly home. That week, Steve took up a secret collection among the other students and professors and presented a Christmas card to this young man. Along with the card was a surprise financial gift of eleven hundred dollars—the exact amount needed for a ticket home for the holidays.

God sets up divine interventions just to bless us! When we are looking for our daily divine appointments, we find more than the excitement of being used by God. When we walk in the Spirit, we will find that God has preordained people to cross our path to be a blessing to us.

A few years ago, I was invited to make a guest appearance as Mrs. USA at the nation's largest health food and product convention. I rarely accept bookings unless I can share about Christ, but I felt in my spirit that God wanted me to go. As the date approached, I began to pray for divine appointments. I knew there would be many unbelievers there, and I wanted to be used by God. There were over two thousand exhibit booths in this massive convention hall; as I traveled the aisles, I saw countless faces and every type of health product you could imagine. My head was spinning and my feet were aching, but I was having the time of my life—all the health food and snack exhibitors were giving out free samples of their tasty products! *This must be heaven!* I thought. *All this fantastic food—and it's healthy, too!*

When my friend Jennifer and I got back to our room, we dumped the bags and bags of loot onto the bed. With wrappers flying, we tore into the goods like a bunch of giggling kids after Halloween. Except this was different. We pigged out on health food!

That night we drifted off to sleep with smiles on our faces. The next morning, I remember looking at Jennifer and laughing, "Look at you! Your eyes are swollen shut!"

"Me?" She shot back. "Look at you! Your eyes are so puffy it looks like you're wearing pillows!"

We both ran to the mirror and gasped in horror. I felt ashamed and embarrassed for overeating like I did, but that didn't solve the puffy-eye problem. My mind raced for a solution. "Quick," I blurted. "There's a sample of eye gel that we got from somewhere yesterday. It's our only hope."

We dug through the pile of samples and food wrappers in our desperate search—hoping that we hadn't accidentally consumed it last night in our feeding frenzy. We finally found the small package and wasted no time in plastering some gel on our eyes.

To our amazement, within minutes the swelling was gone! We looked at each other and knew we had to find out who made this amazing stuff. Easier said than done. Considering the Health Expo had more than one hundred thousand attendees and two thousand exhibit booths, this was going to be like finding a needle in a haystack. I also knew that, because I had obligations to be at the booth of the company that hired me, I wasn't going to be able to spend the day on a vain expedition, hunting for some mysterious, magic eye gel. So, I did the only thing I knew how to do in desperate situations like this that are beyond my control. "Dear God," I prayed as I grabbed Jennifer's hand, "we don't want to be vain, but if it is Your will, please give us a divine appointment with these people."

Within a few minutes, a woman approached me in the crowded walkway at the convention center. "Excuse me," she began. "Are you the Mrs. USA I saw on TV who had the weight problem and overcame drug abuse?"

"Why, yes." I answered.

"I can't believe it!" she continued. "We have a Christian-owned skin care company, and we have been so impressed with your testimony and boldness to share your faith. Would you like to walk with me to our booth? I'd like to give you some skin care samples to try."

We were delighted to go with her, but when we got to her booth, we were absolutely amazed that this was the same company that made the miracle eye gel for which we were searching. It gets better. Not only did we get more samples, but they offered me an opportunity to be a spokesmodel for their line of skin care.

I am often humbly reminded of how much God loves me and wants to order my steps. He carries me during the difficult times, yet also longs to bless me even in the seemingly insignificant things, too. I think God, the Master sculptor, likes to leave His loving handprint on every area of our lives if we let Him. He does this to remind us that we are always in His hands—daily molded with a caring touch into something that is pleasing and useful to Him.

Rest Stop

Write about a divine appointment you had with someone when you least expected it. If you feel led to mail this story to our headquarters, we'd love to read or publish your story in our *Fit for Excellence* newsletter.

14

Finishing Strong

Do you know if you are spiritually healthy? With physical health, it is often hard to tell if someone is really healthy or not. If we have the time and money, we can do tests, take x-rays, and look for toxins.

To determine spiritual health, however, all we need to look for is "fruit." Spiritual fruit, that is. God did not choose us to be ornaments on the wall or trophies on a mantle. He chose us and appointed us to go and bear fruit—fruit that will last. (See John 15:8.) The evidence that we are spiritually fit can be seen by the spiritual fruit we produce. "But the fruit of the Spirit is love, joy, peace, patience, kindness, goodness, faithfulness, gentleness and self-control" (Gal. 5:22–23).

Many of us can look at this fruit and, if we're really truthful, acknowledge that we've thrown these words around a lot. Maybe it wasn't really "godly" love we gave or received. Or perhaps we haven't been experiencing true, perfect peace or joy to the fullest.

What we often see in our lives and others is a worldly "counterfeit"—not a fruit of the Spirit at all. Just as the fruit of a lemon and orange tree look exactly the same when they are immature, the fruit we produce can resemble a cheaper, worldly version when immature. But when we are firmly planted in God and abiding in Him, the Holy Spirit does an amazing work through us by producing healthy, spiritual fruit. Fruit that lasts. The fruit that proves we are spiritually fit.

SPIRITUALLY FIT PEOPLE . . .

- Have power, purpose, and passion for life. They know their place in this world. They don't get distracted by the things of the world because their eyes are set on the things of eternal value.
- Operate in their own gifts and are not jealous of other's gifts. They realize that all the gifts are needed to achieve spiritual excellence.
- Take care of God's temple (their bodies).
- Are free from the bondage of other people's opinion. They are God-pleasers, not people-pleasers.
- Keep their daily divine appointments.
- Give others the freedom to fail.
- Read the Word daily.
- Don't see the obstacles in their life as the end because they know that with God all things are possible.
- Are never too busy to take care of the business of their heavenly Father. They are willing to serve God at any cost.
- Guard their hearts and minds (music, TV, entertainment, magazines, conversations).
- Love God so much that even if He doesn't change their financial situation, heal their body, bring back the spouse that left them, even if *nothing* works out the way they had hoped, the fact that Jesus died for them is enough.

Fix your thoughts on what is true and honorable and right. Think about things that are pure and lovely and admirable. Think about things that are excellent and worthy of praise.

—Philippians 4:8, NLT

Spiritually Fit People Always Finish Strong!

It takes a spiritually fit person to finish strong. Anybody can start something. Very few finish what they start. It really doesn't take much effort to start, but it takes everything that is in you to finish.

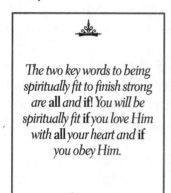

The two key words to being spiritually fit to finish strong are all and if! You will be spiritually fit if you love Him with all your heart and if you obey Him.

It's easy to start college, but it's hard to graduate. It's easy to have a wedding, but it's hard to stay married. It's easy to love a baby, but it's hard to raise a child. It's easy to start a diet, but it's hard to stick with a lifestyle change. It's easy to start a ministry, but it's hard to finish strong when the enemy hits hard.

Spiritually Fit People Don't Quit!

When the world has come against you and you feel like quitting, think of it as an opportunity to earn your P.H.D. (Past Having Doubts). To earn this degree, you'll have to pass all the tests given by the school of life. You'll have to study the textbook (the Bible) and follow the Teacher's example (Jesus). You'll find your Teacher will be totally devoted to helping you earn this degree. He will go through all the tests in life with you, tutoring you at every step of the way.

Once you've completed the courses, you'll be able to graduate. You'll find your P.H.D. to be of great value to you all the days of your life. You'll know your place in this world. You'll have peace that passes human understanding. You'll have the power to finish strong. You'll enjoy your journey!

SPIRITUALLY FIT PEOPLE ARE OBEDIENT!

If we want to see a revival in our land, it will have to start with our own personal obedience. Unless our hearts are pure and our lives are an example, we will not be able to handle the explosion of a revival.

Obedience should be the goal of every Christian. Unless we can prove through our lives that God's way is the right way, then we do not have any credibility with the world. People do not care what we know until they know how much we care.

Our lives are a living Bible for people to see.

Some of the greatest wisdom we can receive was from a man of God during his final days on earth. Moses was chosen by God to deliver God's people out of slavery. Just before he died, he shared the blessings of obedience and the consequences of disobedience:

> The LORD your God will make you successful in everything you do. He will give you many children and numerous livestock, and your fields will produce abundant harvests, for the LORD will delight in being good to you as he was to your ancestors. The LORD your God will delight in you if you obey his voice and keep the commands and laws written in this Book of the Law, and if you turn to the LORD your God with all your heart and soul.
>
> This command I am giving you today is not too

difficult for you to understand or perform. It is not up in heaven, so distant, that you must ask, "Who will go to heaven and bring it down so we can hear and obey it?" It is not beyond the sea, so far away that you must ask, "Who will cross the sea to bring it to us so we can hear and obey it?" The message is very close at hand; it's on your lips and in your heart so that you can obey it.

Now listen! Today I am giving you a choice between prosperity and disaster, between life and death. I have commanded you today to love the LORD your God and to keep his commands, laws, and regulations by walking in his ways. If you do this, you will live and become a great nation, and the LORD your God will bless you and the land you are about to enter and occupy. But if your heart turns away and you refuse to listen, and if you are drawn away to serve and worship other gods, then I warn you now that you will certainly be destroyed. You will not live a long, good life in the land you are crossing the Jordan to occupy.

Today I have given you the choice between life and death, between blessings and curses. I call on heaven and earth to witness the choice you make. Oh, that you would choose life, that you and your descendants might live! Choose to love the LORD your God and to obey him and commit yourself to him, for he is your life.

—DEUTERONOMY 30:9–20, NLT

SPIRITUALLY FIT PEOPLE UNDERSTAND THE CONSEQUENCES OF DISOBEDIENCE

Then my anger will blaze forth against them. I will abandon them, hiding my face from them, and they will be destroyed. Terrible trouble will come down on them, so that they will say, "These disasters have come because God is no longer among us!" At that time I will hide my face from them on account of all the sins they

have committed by worshiping other gods.
—DEUTERONOMY 31:17–18, NLT

"If anyone loves me, he will obey my teaching" (John 14:23). God's love is unconditional, but His promises are not!

We can't expect God to bless us with . . .

- Health without taking care of God's temple.
- Finances without tithing.
- Power without prayer.
- Peace without trust.
- Healing without repentance.
- Victory without accountability.
- Wisdom without God's Word.
- Abundance without obedience.
- An eternal crown without a cross.

SPIRITUALLY FIT PEOPLE KNOW THAT THE AUTHOR AND THE FINISHER OF THEIR FAITH IS JESUS CHRIST!

They know they were created to finish something while they're here on earth. They are committed to finishing strong!

Noah built an ark with no clouds. Abraham left his homeland for a "place he knew not." Gideon had to send his army home (leaving him to fight with only three hundred men). Joshua marched and blew a trumpet. Naaman washed in the muddy Jordan! Daniel worshiped the Lord even in the lion's den.

If my people, who are called by my name, will humble themselves and pray and seek my face and turn from their wicked ways, then will I hear from heaven and will forgive their sin and will heal their land.
—2 CHRONICLES 7:14

Finishing Strong

SPIRITUALLY FIT PEOPLE ARE ON
FIRE FOR GOD!

If nothing changes in our nation except us, we have the power (God's power within us) to restore people's faith in God, rebuild a godly foundation on which to stand, return to the godly principles that protect us, and give the church credibility again.

John Wesley said, "Get on fire for God, and people will come and watch you burn." Let's get burning!

CONCLUSION

I pray that you will do your very best and allow God to do the rest. I pray that you will stay motivated to take care of God's temple, your body. I pray that you will remain real with God so that He can continue to heal your every hurt and share in your every joy. I pray that you will use your God-given gifts to be a present to those around you. I pray you will never lose sight of who you are in Christ, a daughter of the King, a special princess created in His image. I pray you will experience the excitement of your adventures with the King by keeping your daily divine appointments. May He continue to strengthen you in your journey to excellence. My final prayer for you is found in Psalm 20:4–5: "May he give you the desire of your heart and make all your plans succeed. We will shout for joy when you are victorious and will lift up our banners in the name of our God."

I look forward to the day we can celebrate together on the other side of eternity.

> Now glory be to God! By his mighty power at work within us, he is able to accomplish infinitely more than we would ever dare to ask or hope.
> —EPHESIANS 3:20, NLT

175

Fit for Excellence

**God's Design For
Breaking Free From...**

- **Food Addiction**

- **Eating Disorders**

- **Poor Self-Image**

- **Emotional Pain**

- **Depression**

- **Exhaustion**

**More than 30,000 women will attend a
Fit For Excellence Conference this year!**

For more information about attending or hosting a conference in your area, call (602) 407-8789

Order the Fit For Excellence

Audio, Video, Workbook Series

Great for your

- *Sunday school class*
- *Home group*
- *Bible study*
- *Teenage girls*
- *Women's ministry*
- *Church library*

Join the thousands who have been set free from...

- **Food addiction**
- **Eating Disorders**
- **Depression**
- **Emotional Pain**
- **Chronic Fatigue & Exhaustion**
- **Poor Self-Image**

Conference speaker Sheri Rose shares how she lost over 50 pounds and has kept it off for 17 years and teaches how she found victory after struggling for years with Chronic Fatigue Syndrome and a severe eating disorder. She uses humor, fascinating facts, and biblical principles as she shares from the heart a vision of victory for <u>all</u> women.

Randy Carlson
Host of Parent Talk Radio and President of Today's Family Life Communications

" We encourage women's ministry leaders and pastors to incorporate this *"* teaching into their ministries. Those who experience this teaching will be blessed according to I Thessalonians 5:23, *"Now may the God of peace sanctify you completely, and may your whole spirit, soul, and body be preserved blameless at the coming of our Lord Jesus Christ."*

For Orders, Call Toll-free 1•888•777•2439